The *Mahabharata* and Contemporary Indian Novel

The

Mahabharata

and

Contemporary Indian Novel

Shashi Tharoor • Pratibha Ray • S.L. Bhyrappa

Prema Jagannathan

Prestige

an international publishing house

Published by
Prestige Books
C 3/1, Janakpuri
New Delhi 110 058
Ph. 9818755529
email: prestigebooks@gmail.com
website: asiabookclub.com

Associate Office
60/29-45 Parramatta Road,
Concord, NSW 2137
Australia

ISBN: ISBN: 81-7851-069-3

Printed at Chaman Offset Press, New Delhi 110 002

Contents

Foreword
7

Preface
9

Introduction: *The Mahabharata*:
Creative and Critical Traditions
11

The Politics of History:
Shashi Tharoor's *The Great Indian Novel*
49

Draupadi as the Archetypal Victim:
Pratibha Ray's *Yajnaseni*
87

Challenging the Archetypes:
S.L. Bhyrappa's *Parva*
112

Conclusion:
Tradition and Contemporary Relevance
139

Bibliography
155

Foreword

The question of 'canon' in literary studies came up in a big way since the rise of theory from the 1970s. The 'complication' of literary studies caused by the emergence of cultural studies in the last decade of the 20th century made the engagement with 'canon' more fascinating. The challenge to a canon was more in the spirit of questioning the idea of an immutable canon rather than negating the very idea of canon. The emergence of diverse theoretical schools after structuralism and deconstruction has sought to throw into relief hitherto submerged subject positions, such as those of woman, child, worker, slave, inspired by Subaltern Studies. This development has facilitated the efflorescence of a plethora of critical studies which re-search canons in different spheres. Dr. Prema Jagannathan's book is a product of such a critical effort. She has taken up the task of unravelling the specific perspectives of three Indian novels which resist the canonical *Mahabharata*: Shashi Tharoor's use of the epic to offer a political satire of modern India, Pratibha Ray's trenchant feminist reconstruction of the work from the point of view of Draupadi and S.L. Bhyrappa's ruthless attempt to demythologize the story to offer a social critique. In the process we get not just a chance to recall the *Mahabharata* but also hone our reading skills by following the analysis of the chosen books. It is a double bonanza, so to say.

The 'aporias' discovered in Vyasa's book by the three writers result in remaking the 'itihasa' to make it relevant to the contemporary reader. Such an effort is bound to be interesting not only to a native reader but also to those ideologically inclined across cultures because in many cultures today, canons and canonical studies are vigorously being decentred. Prema Jagannathan makes a telling point that all resisting does not efface the original *Mahabharata* but vouchsafes its perennial vibrancy. This is testified to by the recent book on the epic by Gurucharan Das who has delved into its profound complexities even from the point of view of corporate culture. Literary researchers will find Prema's book stimulating.

Professor of English (Retd.)
University of Madras, Chennai

C.T. Indra

Preface

The Indian epics have always held a fascination for me. The *Mahabharata* has been the source of creative insight and inspiration to the modern novelist, who using the ideological framework of the twentieth century seems to reinterpret and deconstruct the epic. P. Lal's two volumes on creative insights into Vyasa's *Mahabharata* provide ample scope for research in this area. Further exploration revealed that in the twentieth century there has not only been a large number of re-renderings but also re-visionings of the text. This merited critical study. The existing corpus is so vast that the study has to be limited to only those works that make a startling departure from the original text of Vyasa.

Shashi Tharoor's *The Great Indian Novel* gives fresh insights into historiography. That history could be untrue and biased makes history itself resemble fiction. Women's issues have been foregrounded in the twentieth century. Pratibha Ray's passionate espousal of the cause of women is seen in *Yajnaseni* which focuses on the plight of Draupadi. The attempts to demythologise the epic by S.L. Bhyrappa in *Parva* is challenging. Through all these deviations the *Mahabharata* emerges as the focal point, a work that conveys to every age the lessons that it needs to learn. This gave me the focus for my study.

Variations in spelling exist. The names of characters have been spelt differently by these novelists. The spelling used by the novelist has been retained in the respective chapter.

I cannot close these prefatory remarks without acknowledging my gratitude to those who have been helpful in the preparation of this book. To acknowledge the valuable guidance and meticulous scrutiny of my work by my supervisor Dr. A. Vishnu Bhat, words are inadequate. My choice of topic called for guidance from a scholar with a rootedness and solid knowledge in the Sanskrit originals and in the literary theories of myth and motif. In these areas, Dr. A. Vishnu Bhat was my perfect mentor. I greatly value the freedom he gave me to pursue my independent line of study.

I am very grateful to the Management, Stella Maris College, Chennai for the award of Teacher fellowship to me. It came at the right time for me to give my whole-hearted attention to academic research and complete it in time, with persistent concentration. My special thanks are due to Dr. Sr. Annamma Philip, Principal, Stella Maris College for her support and understanding in my hour of need

Further, I wish to place on record my deep gratitude to Dr. C.T. Indra, Professor and Head of the Department of English, University of Madras for being a source of inspiration to me. Her valuable guidance and scholarly insights into my area of research have added weight to my study, especially through her clarification of certain key concepts in contemporary critical theory.

I specially thank Dr. Seetha Srinivasan, my former Head of the Department for giving me the fundamental motivation to do research. I am grateful to her for her guidance and valuable suggestions.

I owe my greatest debt of gratitude to my friend and colleague Dr. Padmamalini Sundararaghavan for evincing genuine interest in the successful completion of my research project. The interesting discussions I had with her, gave a sense of focus and direction to my thesis and I can't thank her enough, for her generous gift of time spent with me. Personally, she remains a source of great moral support to me.

I thank my friends and colleagues both in Stella Maris College and other Colleges who were of help and support to me in several ways. I sincerely thank all the members of my family--my son, my husband and my mother-in-law, for their patience and cooperation during the period of my research.

Looking back, I realize that it is only by the grace of God Almighty and all his blessings uncountable that I have been able to complete my study. To Him be all glory for all human endeavours that reach their fruition.

Chapter 1

Introduction
The Mahabharata: Creative and Critical Traditions

Universal in significance, timeless in its appeal, *The Mahabharata* is a veritable treatise on the ethics of choice in every human predicament. It has been generally hailed as the "Fifth Veda" and Vyasa's "Millennial Banquet." It has undergone several recreations through translations, adaptations and transactions by generations of writers. Each recreation or retelling goes to prove the living literary tradition of the epic. Northrop Frye in *Anatomy of Criticism* remarks: "the traditional tales and myths and histories have a strong tendency to stick together and form encyclopedic aggregates [. . .] and in India where the process of transmission was more relaxed, the two traditional epics apparently went on distending themselves for centuries like pythons swallowing sheep" (56). As the epic acquires perpetual growth and enrichment, it assimilates into itself the socio-cultural history of the nation. R.C. Shah in "*The Mahabharata* as the Inspiration for Living Literary Tradition" in Dandekar's *The Mahabharata Revisited* traces the history of the creative renderings of the epic. He endorses Sri Aurobindo's statement that the epic has become the creation and expression of a collective national mind, which also proves the close link between the epic and the history of the nation (245).

Any upheaval in the society necessitates a review of the past. The two World Wars have caused so great a devastation that the need to search for a force that binds humanity together is felt more than ever before. R.C Shah says that every period of social transformation tends to exact an effort of reorientation towards the cultural past of the community as a vital ingredient of the struggle to face the present and shape the future (246). Several writers have attempted to recreate the epic to reflect the spirit of the times and this is a sure proof of the inherent richness of the epic. V.S. Sethuraman in "Literature after Theory: A Case Study" published in *Indian Journal of American Studies* says, "a conscious search for retelling of old stories and discovering of parallel situations have added a new dimension to our cultural and critical discourse" (34). Some writers have re-rendered the epic in their own idiom but always with a nostalgia for the old. Some have chosen to deviate from Vyasa's epic to express their own ideological concerns. They fall into two broad categories of retellings and fictional renderings. The word *retell* is used in the sense of a faithful re-rendering of the epic in the writer's own diction and style. On the other hand, fictional renderings signify the creative artist's freedom to recast the events and to reinterpret the characters to serve the professed intent of the novelist. There had been a wide range of mode of narration in different literary genres. A brief review of the available re-renderings is also given in this chapter followed by a review of extant criticism.

Considering the vastness of the existing corpus, the present study has been limited to Shashi Tharoor's *The Great Indian, Novel*, S.L. Bhyrappa's *Parva* and Pratibha Ray's *Yajnaseni*. *The Great Indian Novel* has been written in English. *Parva* originally written in Kannada has been translated into English by K. Raghavendra Rao. *Yajnaseni*, an Oriya novel has been translated into English by Pradeep Bhattacharya. The works are worth a serious study on account of the new perspectives that emerge from them and the study does not propose to assess them as translations. These three works have fictionalized the *Mahabharata* from a non-traditional perspective. The perspective in these works has been shaped by the shifts in the social, political and cultural milieu of the twentieth century. Fictionalizing is a process that involves recasting of events, reinterpretation of characters, deviations and distortions.

This study examines how the process of fictionalizing the epic in contemporary times has resulted in a reinforcement of its relevance. It does not make an attempt at presenting the glory of the epic by expounding the moral and ethical values found in it. Such an exercise will be a redundant endeavour. All the three works fall outside the traditional parameters of assessment of the epic and they are shaped by the distinct socio-political concerns of the writers. Some of the concepts of contemporary critical theories that aid the study of fictionalizing the epic are selectively used. No single approach is consistently applied to all the texts. The approach adopted for each text is dependent on the socio-political concerns of the author and will necessarily vary.

Reacting against the immense popularity of the televised *Ramayana*, Romila Thapar calls attention to the plurality of the *Ramayana* in Indian history as quoted by Paula Richman in *Many Ramayanas*.

> The *Ramayana* does not belong to any one moment in history for it has its own history which lies embedded in the many versions which were woven around the theme at different times and places. [. . .] The appropriation of the story by a multiplicity of groups meant a multiplicity of versions through which the social aspirations and ideological concerns of each group were articulated. The story in these versions included significant variations which changed the conceptualization of character, event and meaning. (4)

Just like the multiple tellings of the *Ramayana*, an array of re-renderings of its twin epic of the *Mahabharata* displays a scintillating variety and richness. In this context it is worth quoting the view of A.K. Ramanujan on the various tellings of the *Ramayana*. He says that the *Ramayana* tradition can be likened to a pool of signifiers that include the plot, characters, names, geography, incidents and relations and argues that each *Ramayana* can be seen as crystallization. He says, "these various texts not only relate to prior texts directly, to borrow or refute but they relate to each other through a common code or common pool. Every author, if one may hazard a metaphor, dips into it and brings out a unique crystallization, a new text with a unique texture and a fresh context (Richman 46). A.K. Ramanujan's findings are equally applicable to the different versions of the *Mahabharata* and the three texts chosen for study provide fresh insights into the epic.

A study of the process of fictionalization leading to either re-assessment or distortion of the epic necessitates the recognition of a canonical text or a standard text against which the deviations have to be discussed. The recognition of such a basic text raises issues in relation to authorship and authenticity to the text. Traditional belief points to Vyasa as the author of the *Mahabharata*. P.L. Bhargava, in *Retrieval of History from Puranic Myths*, says that the *Mahabharata* is popularly believed to be a creation of Vyasa.

> The internal evidence of the great epic indicates that it was originally called *Jaya* since it narrated only the events leading to the victory of the Pandavas over the Kauravas. This original poem probably consisted of only 8800 verses. These verses, however, appeared so intricate after the lapse of some centuries that the need for amplifications was felt. The poem thus swelled to the size of 24000 verses and came to be called *Bharata*. There were, however, still no episodes in it. Its popularity eventually led to its conversion into a compendium of knowledge with the addition of all kinds of episodes and didactic matter raising its bulk to 1,00,000 verses. In the final form it received the name *Mahabharata*. (89).

Similar options have been expressed by several critics on the text of the *Mahabharata*. Irawati Karve in *Yuganta* has recognized the accretive nature of the epic.

> The word *Mahabharata* forces us to recognize stages in the making of the poem. Perhaps, there was a simpler and less extensive story called Bharata and then, by century long accretions, it became a maha (integral) Bharata (book about the descendants of Bharata). The present version of the book, however, lets one know that there was a still an earlier time when the narration had the much shorter and simpler name, *Jaya* (Victory). This means that in its earliest form the narration was a poem of triumph, and told of the victory of a particular king over his rival kinsmen. (1)

Her supposition is based on the idea that the word Vyasa as a title meant 'arranger,' a man who throws together or orders. She says, "from the *Mahabharata* story we know that his own name was Krishna (the black) Dvaipayana (born on the island). If we take into consideration this tradition, then perhaps, Vyasa was not the original composer of the story but the man who might have taken it as told by the suta bards and arranged it" (7).

The views of Bhargava and Karve point to an assumption that the *Mahabharata* was compiled by Vyasa and that he should have been influenced by the oral tradition of reciting stories by Suta poets (Bards). Krishna Chaitanya in his literary study of *the Mahabharata* also refers to such suppositions regarding Vyasa's contribution to the text of 1,00,000 couplets which could not be attributed to a single creative consciousness.

In Chaitanya's opinion also, the idea of collective authorship is attributed to the *Mahabharata.* He says: "Tradition refers to a first version, the *Jaya* of 8800 couplets, a second, the *Bharata*, of 24,000 couplets, and the third and final, the *Mahabharata* in its present form with over 1,00,000 couplets. He thinks that this process of growth may have taken centuries. It is not possible to think in terms of a poet, a single creative consciousness, to whom we can attribute the poem. He further states that there is no specific reference in the *Mahabharata* to Vyasa as the editor of the Vedas:

> The opening chapter of the Adi Parvan does make the claim that the epic gives the essence of all the four Vedas, but this is a wholly different thing. On the other hand, there is a pointed mention in the Adi Parvan that he re-edited the epic itself several times [. . .] but the point is that there is great emphasis on the work done as a Vyasa or editor. The primate work too was one of editorship though one of supremely creative editings and this must been a lifetime undertaking. The contemporaries of the poet could easily have got into the habit of referring to him as Vyasa. In later times, he was regarded by mistake as the editor of the Vedas. By long usage Vyasa has become as good as a personal name and we too shall use it that way (xiii).

Sir Aurobindo is of the opinion that the original epic consisted for 26400 slokas but the final for runs to 1,00,000 (9).

> Astau sloka—sahasrani astau sloka—satanica /
> Aham, vedmi suko vetti sanjayo vetti va na va //

This sloka by Vyasa hints at the collaborative efforts put in by him, his son Suka, and Sanjaya to transmit the epic orally to the succeeding generation. According to Aurobindo, western Indologists have given a faulty interpretation of this sloka, in that they thought that the sloka is intended to tell the readers the total number of slokas contained in the original text. But Vyasa himself says that he wrote the *Mahabharata* in 1,00,000 slokas and as such he calls it *Sata-Sahasri*. Therefore, what Vyasa means to say in the above sloka is that he, Suka, and Sanjaya committed to memory 26,400. The rest of the text was distributed among the disciples of Vyasa (9).

Ancient Indians mastered the art of learning by committing to memory several thousand verses, formulas and maxims. It has been said that Panini's towering masterpiece *Ashtadhyayi* is composed in the form of a string of short statements, no doubt to facilitate memorization (Rajaram and Frawley 137). The oral tradition of learning through discussions, debates and logistic dialogues (tarka) widened their perspective and made acquisition of knowledge a pleasurable experience. Sidney's sixteenth century concept of instruction and delight had been actively put into practice by the ancient Indian Scholars. These techniques of learning and memorization, which the west now recognized as superlearning-techniques, are part of the rich (cultural) heritage of India. David Frawley and Rajaram point out, "Vedic civilization was predominantly an indigenous evolution. All the ingredients necessary for human development are right there in the heartland going back to time immemorial" (208). It is a figment of the imagination of the Indologists, who are unfamiliar with the ancient Indian methodology of learning that discredits Vyasa as a mere compiler and not the sole author of the *Mahabharata*.

These observations point to the traditional assumptions of Vyasa as the author of the epic endorsed by a general acceptance of such a belief for practical reasons. The study refers to the final form of the text called the *Mahabharata* having 1,00,000 couplets commonly attributed to Vyasa as the basic text against which deviations and distortions are discussed. The earliest English translation by M.N. Dutt in seven volumes based on the Calcutta edition of northern recension is used for all the practical purposes of reference. Dutt's edition is the only available sloka to sloka translation in English. The transliterated verses of the Sanskrit text of

Vyasa are given separately wherever necessary. Since the English translation and the Sanskrit text of Vyasa are based on different critical editions, the sloka numbers do not always correspond. But thematically, both texts refer to the same episode or event.

V.S. Sethuraman in "Literature after Theory: A Case Study" refers to *The Mahabharata* as a canonical text. The word canon is defined as 'the body of texts culturally perceived as pre-eminent for their aesthetic quality and their imputed truth. Ecclesiastically, it refers to works accepted as having divine authority" (Pam Morris 195). *The Random House Dictionary of the English Language* defines "canon" as "the body of rules, principles or standards accepted as axiomatic and universally binding in a field of study or art; neo-classical canon, Literature, the works of an author which have been accepted as authentic." Going by these definitions, the *Mahabharata* canon includes the authorized, accepted text of Vyasa, with 1,00,000 couples, culturally considered as pre-eminent for its aesthetic quality and imputed truth. It is this text that has served as a canonical text for generation of writers who have attempted to retell the epic.

The recognition of a basic text in order to set off the deviations raises issues relating to authorship, influences and evolutionary nature of the text itself. Chaitanya's remark that the opening chapter of the epic which claims that it contains the essence of all the four Vedas reveals the earliest influences on the epic itself. The idea of influence of the Vedas has been well illustrated by Sethuraman in his "Resonance and Intertextuality" in *A Way of Leaving So as to Say*. He observes that the metaphor, the rhythm and the philosophical implications of the comments on the nature of man, his mortality, found in the *Bhagavad Gita* are precisely those of the earlier Upanishadic text *Kathopanishad*. He says, "we have here not so much an instance of echo or allusion as of Intertextuality" (159). In the same essay he refers to the blurring of distinctions in the last few decades of the century and influence has been replaced by Intertextuality. Obviously a study of fictionalization of *Mahabharata* has necessitated an examination of concepts such as influence, Intertextuality, role of the author and so on, in which there are echoes of some of the current literary doctrines of western critical theories.

Sethuraman discusses Harold Blooms' claim in *The Anxiety of Influence* that every text is an intertext, and says that Bloom sees the desire to evade earlier writing as a central motivation in literary production.

> Every poet is influenced by his precursor poet, but he would consciously try 'to kill' the precursor poet. No strong poem alludes to another and what looks like overt allusions and echoes in strong poems are disguises for darker relationship. Intertextuality seems to be more complex. The term was coined by Julia Kristeva to denote the interdependence of any one literary text on or inter-relationship with all those that have gone before it. It implies that a text is just a mosaic of quotations. Texts absorb and transform one another. (Marathe et al 154)

It is true that literary artists cannot escape the influence of their predecessors. The concept of Intertextuality has been put to constant use in the Indian literary tradition. It has been a technique of comparison and commentary in Indian poetics. The west recognized this concept centuries later and has theorized an ancient Indian literary practice. In India the influence of Vyasa, Valmiki and Kalidasa on successive generations of writers is tremendous. Similarly Homer, Virgil and Seneca have wielded great influence on English writers. Among the English writers, Spenser has influenced Milton. Marlowe's plays bear the influence of Seneca. Eliot's poetry reveals the influence of both western and Indian literary traditions. A study of influences and parallels is in fact a branch of comparative literature, a discipline by itself.

Influence could be at different levels; thematic, structural, stylistic and so on. Several writers have retold the earlier works from different points of view. The theme of the *Mahabharata* has been the nucleus around which poems, plays and novels have been built up. Among the contemporary works *Arjun* by Sunil Gangopadhyay is a novel that artistically exploits the theme of the *Mahabharata*. Peter Brooks has dramatized the epic. In the Indian literary tradition itself, it has a strong impact on the writers. A novelist like Raja Rao has creatively adopted the Puranic tradition of story telling in his novel *Kanthapura*. Several ancient myths have been the source of many literary works. But the re-renderings of the Indian epics—both the *Ramayana* and the *Mahabharata*—are not born out of the burden of anxiety. It is a deliberate, conscious effort at adapting the earlier works to a different context. The works chosen for the present study are also deliberate reworking of the epic *Mahabharata* to comment on the contemporary situation. These writers have consciously established links with the epic in terms of form, content and narrative technique.

The concept of Intertextuality has been promoted by several writers with variations. Harold Bloom and Julia Kristeva have used the term to show the interdependence of literary texts and a network of textual relations. Poststructuralists have used the term to disrupt notions of stable meaning and objective interpretation. Graham Allen in his Critical Idiom Series on *Intertextuality* points out that Barthes uses the term to challenge long-held assumptions concerning the role of the author in the production of meaning (3). Raman Selden, giving a critique of poststructuralism, refers to Barthes's essay *S/Z* (1970) and says that Barthes rejects the myth of uncovering the structure of a text because each text possesses a "difference." Each text refers back differently to the infinite sea of the already written (78). The reader is capable of producing multiple meaning. As Selden Raman says "The I which reads is already itself a plurality of other texts" (78).

It is true of the Indian epic that each text refers back to the infinite sea of the already written as it contains the essence of the Vedas and the Upanishads and it can be equally applied to the reworkings of the epic too. The reader's potential of plurality of texts is borne out of the fact that every reader is inspired to take on the role of the writer to provide fresh creative insights into the epic. In this context the earliest title of the epic *Jaya* celebrating the victory at Kurukshetra can be considered as an elaborate metaphor. Kuru in Sanskrit means to do/ make/ create and Kshetra can mean the place/ body/ mind. As an extended metaphor it implies that the concept of victory is relative and is perceived by the mind. Milton in his *Paradise Lost* echoes this idea when he says: "The

Mind is its own place and in itself / Can make heaven of hell and a hell of heaven" (I: 254-5).

In this context it is appropriate to quote Vanashree Tripathi's remark on the nature of the epic *Mahabharata*. She says in her "Polysemy at the Dead End: Shashi Tharoor's *The Great Indian Novel*" that the *Mahabharata* is an infinitely scriptable text (Pathak 116). The great epic of India finds echoes in Barthes's distinction between readerly and writerly texts. According to Barthes, if the text discourages the reader to produce his own meaning, then it is a closed text. Such a text makes the reader a consumer and the text that encourages the reader to bring out multiple meanings makes him a producer. The former is called a readerly / legible text and the latter is called a writerly/ scriptable text. According to Roland Barthes, an ideal text is "a galaxy of signifiers" (Selden 78). Such concepts are not new to the critics of the *Mahabharata*. M.F. Salat refers to an observation by V.S. Sukhthankar on the richness of the epic that it is one of the most inspiring monuments of the world and an inexhaustible mine for the investigation of the religion, mythology, legend, philosophy, law, custom and political and social institutions of India (127).

The idea of multiple meanings is suggestive of comparison with poststructuralist concept of meaning and the role of the author. It is Roland Barthes who asserted the autonomy of the literary text in "The Death of the Author." He says that a text is made of multiple writings, drawn from many cultures and entering into mutual relations of dialogue, parody, contestation, but there is one place where this multiplicity is focused and that place is the reader, not, as was hitherto said, the author (Rice and Waugh 118). Barthes's ideas of the text, author and meaning are further strengthened by Derrida's discussion on the reading of a text. Kathleen Wheeler and C.T. Indra in *Explaining Deconstruction* observe that Derrida's writing indicates the necessity for a thoroughly self-conscious reading, one that subjects its own assumptions to close scrutiny, not just the presumed text. In so doing, not only is reading itself (as traditionally conceived) subverted; the concept of the text along with traditional readings is also subverted. Contradictory readings are shown always to inhabit a single text, thereby deflecting the goal in traditional reading, of closure, univocal meaning and truth (1).

Deconstruction can be seen to work within the body of traditional criticisms itself. The text has inherent unresolvability which leads to a body of interpretation growing around it. This received opinion can be utilized to point out the inconsistencies and contradictions in the text itself deconstructing it.

The poststructuralist's preoccupation with reading has opened up new avenues of criticism and interpretation. Geoffrey Hartman in *Criticism in the Wilderness* points out the new approaches of Criticism such as revision, reinterpretation and rewriting. Hartman denies that criticism reveals any absolute knowledge, but only the nature of the text as infinite, undecidable and interminable—a web of texts, intertexts and interpretations—the harder we try to interpret or decode a text, the more indeterminate it becomes (Wheeler & Indra 7). Such a view explains the status of the *Mahabharata* as an inexhaustible mine of literary richness unfolding infinite possibilities of interpretations.

The radical departure from traditional criticism is further reinforced by Derrida's concept of deconstruction. Wheeler & Indra rightly pointed out that Derrida devised new tactics which were aimed at challenging traditional methods and practices in literary criticism and in philosophy (3). He challenged the accepted borders between philosophy, history, literature, criticism autobiography, sociology and so on, mixing genres, styles and themes (33). Such a strategy of mixing disciplines and genres is true of Shashi Tharoor's *The Great Indian Novel* where the novelist cuts across the borders between history and literature and also mixes the two different genres, the epic and fiction by superimposing the structure of the epic on his satirical fiction.

Raman Selden in *Practising Theory and Reading Literature: An Introduction* says that Derrida takes upon himself to show how impossible it is for us to escape the differential nature of language or to extricate ourselves from the "aporias" of discourse, that is, the undecidable flow and counterflow of all signification (88). The principle of undecidability and indeterminacy of signification, underlines Tharoor's concept of history in his *The Great Indian Novel*.

The early phase of poststructuralism, according to Peter Barry, seems to license, and revel in the endless free play of meanings and the escape from all forms of textual authority. In his review of "Poststructuralism and Deconstruction," Peter Barry observes that Derrida sees in modern times a particular intellectual event which constitutes a radical break from past ways of thought. He says, "the event concerns the decentring of our intellectual universe. Prior to this event the existence of a norm or centre in all things was taken for granted" (66). He adds further that all along western norms of dress, behaviour, architecture, intellectual outlook have provided a firm centre against which deviations, aberrations, variations could be detected and identified as 'Other' and marginal. In the twentieth century, however "these centres were destroyed or eroded; sometimes this was caused by historical events—such as the way the First World War destroyed the illusion of steady material progress" (67).

The poststructuralist concepts such as the death of the author, the endless free play of meanings and the freedom from textual authority are evidently seen to be at work in the numerous attempts to retell the classics of world literature. The two great Indian epics the *Ramayana* and the *Mahabharata* have been exerting great influence, on the writers, as a living tradition.

The process of decentring of the structure involves a reversal of the binary oppositions forming the metaphysical framework of Western thought such as soul-body, being-non-being, good-bad, content-form, speech-writing, masculine-feminine and so on. Raman Selden says that the deconstructor proceeds by reversing the hierarchy, not perversely but by discerning a chink in the discourse which allows this reversal. Finally, the newly asserted hierarchy is itself displaced and is not allowed to install a new truth of structural fixity (89).

Shashi Tharoor seems to admit the fact that his own text might be displaced when he says at the end of the novel that he might have told the story "from a completely mistaken perspective" and that he "must retell it" (418). If the reversal of the binary oppositions victor/ victim is seen to be at work in Tharoor's deconstruction of the epic and history, the newly asserted hierarchy is likely to undergo a similar process. Derrida himself does not rule out the possibility of thinking outside such terms in his "Structure, Sign and Play in the Discourse of Human Sciences" (Sethuraman 294) Derrida has coined the term "differance" to convey the deferral nature of meaning. As Peter Barry says, texts previously regarded as unified artistic artefacts are shown to be fragmented, self-divided, and centre-less. They always turn out to be representative of monstrous births predicted at the end of "Structure, Sign and Play" (68). The notion of monstrous births and rebirths of a text is the operating principle of several creative insights into the *Mahabharata*.

According to Wheeler and Indra, Derrida and Barthes were to a large extent engaged in a mode of writing that was structurally, stylistically, generically, thematically and academically a genuine rupture with tradition (41). This concept of rupture with tradition or breaking away from tradition is the creative principle of the three primary texts chosen for study that seem to retell the story of the *Mahabharata* from a non-traditional perspective by fictionalizing the epic. Bhyrappa's *Parva* seems to reverse the binary opposition of the terms 'sacred' and 'secular' by reinterpreting the events and the characters through the device of demythologizing. Pratibha Ray in *Yajnaseni* presents the story of the epic from the point of view of Draupadi taking up the cause of the women and the oppressed who have been so long marginalized in the society. Tharoor's *The Great Indian Novel* fictionalizes the epic reversing the hierarchy of the victor-victim in both the epic and history, ultimately making the novel a political satire.

Tharoor draws significant parallels between the ancient epic and modern Indian history in terms of events and characters. The two different disciplines, literature and history co-exist and interact with each other as two texts. The reader is provided a parallel reading of the two texts enabling him to interrogate the past. Such a parallel existence of the two texts, with equal weightage informing and interrogating each other is suggestive of a new historicist approach challenging a conservative assessment of both the epic and history.

Shashi Tharoor's investigations and interrogations of history and the epic presuppose a kind of skepticism involved in the popular conceptions of both history and the epic. It is possible to interpret the novel from the perspective of postmodernism strengthened by deconstruction.

The views of the poststructuralists seem to overlap the concerns of the postmodernists. They not merely overlap but seem to mutually strengthen each other. It will be useful to briefly study the salient features of postmodernism. Postmodernism is basically an attempt at redefining cultural discourses by asserting the need to recall the past to highlight it and subvert it. Referring to the theory of postmodernism in *The Politics of Postmodernism* Lynda Hutcheon says that in general terms it takes the form of self-conscious self-contradictory and self-undermining statement (1). Postmodernism is both a continuation and a contradiction of modernism.

In the same way the novels chosen for the study can be seen as both a continuation and a contradiction of the original epic. There is a blurring of distinction between the sacred and the secular, the victor and the victim, high art and low art in these works. The body of literature arising out of the great epic *The Mahabharata* seems to interrogate the past. The texts interacting with each other have obliterated all the boundaries of hierarchical terms. Referring to the relationship between poststructuralism and postmodernism Raman Selden says that "despite the diversity of trends within each, there is no doubt that poststructuralist thought is to some extent a body of reflections upon the same issues which concern postmodern culture as understood by critics such as Ihab Hassan, Jean Francois Lyotard, Frederic Jameson and Gerald Graff" (72). He says that the postmodern experience stems from a profound sense of ontological uncertainty. He claims, that the questioning of all depth models, the decentering of the world and the self, the rejection of elitist aesthetics and experimental formalisms, the disruption of all discursive boundaries, the obliteration of the frontiers between high culture and low culture and between art and commodity and the resistance to meaning and interpretation, are all themes of poststructuralism (*Ibid.*).

It is true that there is a resistance to meaning as a plurality of vision marks the writings of the authors chosen for study and many more creative re-renderings of the *Mahabharata*.

The vivid portrayal of the scenes of death and decay, multiple voices moaning and groaning, overlapping and intersecting each other, utter chaos and gloom prevailing over and above a mood of jubilation in the victor's camp, all these with a sense of waste towards the end in Bhyrappa's *Parva*, are all of great significance for a society torn asunder by two world wars. The novel strikes a postmodern note at the end. Contemporary fiction best reflects contemporary reality. Cultural historians point out profound links between the nuclear threat of the technologically advanced world and the global phenomenon of fragmented culture. The distinction between high culture and low culture is wiped out leading to the hegemony of commercial culture. Peter Barry says that the modernist laments fragmentations whilst the postmodernist celebrates it (84). A plurality of vision marks the writings of the postmodernists.

Postmodernists encourage free mixing of literary genres and highlight texts of hybridity. Rushdie's *Midnight's Children* fits the description of a hybrid text, a typical postmodern novel which works to foreground the totalizing impulse of western imperialistic modes of history-writing by confronting it with indigenous Indian models of History (Hutcheon 65). Rushdie seems to be the influence behind *The Great Indian Novel* of Tharoor. Influence of the predecessor poet is evident in all revisionist works. Sethuraman asserts that a novel like *The Great Indian Novel* could only have been written after the deconstructive turn that rhetorical critical discourse has taken since Derrida (31). Besides Derrida's theory, other influences are at work in Tharoor's novel; but yet Tharoor's novel cannot be called imitative or derivative of the predecessor artists. Harold Bloom in *The Anxiety of Influence* says that "poetic influence need not make poets less original as often it makes them more original, though not therefore necessarily better" (7).

Tharoor's creative use of the technique makes him more original than his predecessor.

In the process of fictionalizing the epic, the Indian writers consciously mix the Eastern and Western literary tradition. Bhyrappa claims that he adopts the stream of consciousness technique in his *Parva* to explore the psyche of some of the major characters. But there seems to be a great deal of difference between Joycean use of the device and Bhyrappa's conscious employment of the same device. In Joyce the stream of consciousness refers to the illogical sequence of thoughts flowing from the mind of the individual. Bhyrappa has oversimplified the term to refer to the reminiscences and recollection of a character which are identified with the technique of flashback narration. However, the employment of certain artistic strategies (like grafting from traditions that are diametrically opposed to each other) creates an impression of hybridity. According to what Mark Currie states in *Postmodern Narrative Theory*, narratological theory itself has undergone a transition in the 1980s (1). The transition implies the significance of the active role of the reader.

The issues raised by the poststructuralists are by no means new to the body of criticism on the *Mahabharata*. In fact, the epic *Mahabharata* itself raises crucial questions about the role of the author, about the content whether it is history or myth or legend, whether or not Vyasa is a poet or a witness to history, to what extent Vyasa has fictionalized history and how authentic the text of Vyasa is. The encyclopedic nature of the epic leaves the critic bewildered and no conclusions have been arrived at in answer to these issues. By and large the basic situation and the major characters involved in it are accepted by a majority of writers who have attempted retelling, revisioning or fictionalizing the epic. But the writers by their ingenuity and imagination have been given a new thrust to the events or have chosen to reinterpret the characters from a new perspective in conformity with the times.

The women characters of the *Ramayana* and the *Mahabharata* have been a source of perennial interest to the creative artists. The characters of Sita, Savitri, Gandhari and Draupadi are as important as those of the heroes in the epics. Therefore, the writers have found it a rewarding experience to interpret and reinterpret these women characters from a feminist perspective in their works. The lives of Sita, Gandhari and Draupadi raise certain vital issues that are relevant to the twentieth century women. *Yajnaseni* of Pratibha Ray expresses serious concerns about the discrimination of women in the society. While fictionalizing the predicament of Draupadi from a twentieth century perspective, the novelist tries to expose the injustice and inequality to which women have been subjected for a long time. The issues raised by the novelist invite comparison with the preoccupations of the feminists.

Feminist movement in India is an offshoot of western feminism though it started as a suffrage movement in the west. Feminists realized there were greater issues than gaining the vote. According to western feminists, women are oppressed by the patriarchal culture. Pam Marris in *Literature and Feminism* defines feminism as "a political perception based on two fundamental premises: (1) that gender difference is the foundation of a structural inequality between women and men, by which women suffer systematic social injustice and (2) that the inequality between the sexes is not the result of biological necessity but is produced by the cultural construction of gender differences. This perception provides feminism with its double agenda to understand the social and psychic mechanisms, that construct and perpetuate gender inequality, and then to change them" (1). Virginia Woolf is generally considered to be the founding mother of feminist theory. Much before Woolf, Henrik Ibsen had championed the cause of women in his *A Doll's House.* Woolf's critical treatise, *A Room of One's Own*, exposes the deplorable conditions under which women live and suffer. Women have been denied certain basic rights as freedom, education and economic independence in a patriarchal society.

Pratibha Ray's *Yajnaseni* raised the vexed issue of her not being given the freedom to have her say with regard to her marriage with the Pandava brothers. She is annoyed that she is expected to conform to the wishes of Yudhishtir and his brothers. Yajnaseni's furious outbursts are a craving for the freedom of the woman as an individual.

In *A Room of One's Own*, Virginia Woolf puts forth the idea that women have been the victims of a male-dominated society and they have perpetually to act as the looking glass for men to reflect their notions of women. Woolf says, "women have served all these centuries as looking glasses possessing the magic and delicious power of reflecting the figure of man at twice its nature size. For if she begins to tell the truth, the figure in the looking glass shrinks" (37). Virginia Woolf has also highlighted the difficulties faced by women creative artists. But it is interesting to note that she expresses an androgynous vision of creativity.

Pratibha Ray's Yajnaseni has none of the inhibitions about expressing female passion. She does not conceal her passion for Arjun. Such a depiction seems to bear similarity to Woolf's opinion expressed in *Professions for Women* where she refers to the "taboo about expressing female passion. The attempts to write about the experiences of women therefore were aimed at discovering linguistic ways for describing the contrived life of women and she believed that when women finally achieved social and economic equality with men, there would be nothing to prevent them from freely developing their artistic talents." (Selden 209)

Simone de Beauvoir's *The Second Sex* has made significant contribution to feminist theory. She points out the narrow, prejudiced definitions of a woman as a womb, an ovary an object or as the other in relation to man in her very first chapter (36). Her contention is that women have been biologically, psychologically and economically discriminated against. She conceives woman as hesitating between the role of object, 'the other' which is offered her and the assertion of her liberty (83). She insists that a woman be defined as a human being in quest of values in a world of values, a world in which it is indispensable to know the economic and social structure (83). Yajnaseni protests against woman treated as a commodity. "Is woman a part of immovable property"? (235) This question of identity is dealt with by several other feminists such as Betty Friedan and Kate Millett.

Betty Friedan's *The Feminine Mystique* (1963) also highlights the conditions of the oppressed women and sees the majority of women trapped in domestic chores. Mirian Schneir in the *Vintage*

Book of Feminism says that Betty Friedan identified the problem of women as the problem of identity, which lay behind and unspoken for many years (49). Referring to the lack of awareness of American Women about their own problems, Friedan says: "their only dream was to be perfect wives and mothers (. . .) they gloried in their role as women" (53).

Dale Spender's *Man-Made Language* obviously suggests that women were oppressed by even language that is dominated by men. Hardly is there any reference to linguistic bias against women in the Indian context where social and cultural issues form the debates about the status of women. The practice of male domination based on sexuality is emphatically denounced by Kate Millett in her *Sexual Politics*. She analyses a few passages from Jean Genet's works and observes, "Sex is deep at the heart of our troubles, Genet is urging and unless we eliminate the most pernicious of our systems of oppression, unless we go to the very centre of the sexual politic and its sick delirium of power and violence, all our efforts at liberation will only land us again in the same primordial stews (Schneir 144). Millett squarely puts the blame on patriarchal culture.

In this context it is worth considering Krishna Chaitanya's observation of Karna's comments on Draupadi:

> Draupadi's situation never ceased to intrigue Karna. He really seems to have felt that she had a phenomenal libido though, when he said in the Kaurava assembly that she could now find fulfillment with a hundred husbands, he was being extremely ungenerous. But Karna, here, may have been cherishing some animosity.

It is evident here that the epic throws some hints about the aspect of sexuality and that the epic heroine proves her domination over men based on sexuality, a kind of refutation of male superiority over the female. Karna seems to be having what Mary Wollstonecraft calls "mistaken notions of beauty and female excellence" (Schneir 14). Schneir calls Wollstonecraft's "A Vindication of the Rights of Woman" an epoch making call-to-arms as early as 1972 itself (Schneir XVI). Wollstonecraft raised the consciousness of women by saying "If . . . [women] be really capable of acting like rational creatures, let them not be treated like slaves; or like the brutes who are dependent on the reason of man, when they associate with him" (12). Mary Wollstonecraft and Betty Friedan belong to the group of Liberal feminists who demand equality of civil liberties for women and equal opportunities.

Some of the statements attributed to Shakuni and Bhim in Pratibha Ray's *Yajnaseni* seem to deny equality to women. Shakuni says that the greatest sin of a woman is to try to be learned. Bhim wants woman to be "obedient" to her husband. But Shakuni comes to stay in the palace of Hastinapur in order to protect his sister Gandhari. Bhim devotes himself to protecting the honour of Draupadi whenever there is a threat to her modesty from lustful men. The statements of Shakuni and Bhim are not born out of any conviction but are the outbursts of prejudice against the rival party or temperamental misdemeanor.

Marxist feminists believe that class distinctions and patrilineal inheritance rights are the causes of discrimination against women. Shulamith Firestone in "The Dialectic of Sex: The Case of Feminist Revolution" sees class struggle itself as the consequence of an oppressive biological condition (Schneir 256).

Though class struggles exist in India, there is an increasing awareness of the importance of economic independence to a woman. In India, the Hindu Succession Act concedes women equal rights but the inclusion of the provision, allowing a person to will away to anyone's favour he prefers enables fathers to deny these rights to their daughters. But the works chosen for study do not deal with Marxist Feminism or gynocriticism.

Feminists also examine the problem of women's writing and Gynocriticism. Sandra Gilbert and Susan Gubar in *The Madwoman in the Attic* and Elaine Showalter in *A Literature of Their Own* analyze the writings of women and bring out the differences from the points of view of women's experience.

Yet another approach to the study of the discrimination against women is the psychoanalytic method. Bhyrappa seems to explore the psyche of some of the women characters of the *Mahabharata* and his imaginative comprehension of their psyche throws light on the marital unhappiness of these women. This has been exclusively dealt with in the chapter on *Parva*. Psychoanalytic critics are influenced by the theories of Freud. French feminists such as Julia Kristeva and Helene Cixous discuss the relationship between female sexuality and literary productivity. They also disapprove of the situation of woman being relegated to the background as the Other.

African-American and Third world feminists such as Alice Walker and Barbara Johnson are deeply concerned with the problem of identity complicated by race and sexuality.

It is obvious that the issues raised by many of the western feminists relate to identity, gender bias, denial of equal opportunities, language-based oppression, discrimination on the basis of biological differences, aggravated by class and racial distinction. These feminists also highlight the problems of women creative writers.

But the Indian situation is different. A historical perspective of the position of women in India gives an ideal picture of their status. Even in the ancient Vedic society, men and women played complementary roles. In the performance of any ritual or religious ceremony, a man cannot begin anything until the woman lights the fire. An Indian woman is not merely the wife of a man but his friend and advisor; while nursing him she becomes even a mother to him. But it has been often said that a woman is a dependent on man throughout her life. Since a woman is biologically vulnerable to assaults on her modesty, she needs that kind of protection from men.

If the spirit of an ideal is missed or ignored, then the system promoting such an ideal starts degenerating. In India, all the well-meaning practices have been abused and the security of women was threatened with the invasion of Moghuls followed by the advent of the British. To cite an example, Varnasrama dharma recognized and respected the aptitude of the individual for a particular vocation and this was abused in the later day as an evil, perpetrating caste distinctions. The dowry system originated as a compensation for denial of inheritance rights to women; in course of time it degenerated into a social evil.

Though women's issues have been foregrounded in the twentieth century India, the outlook of Indian women is basically different from that of the Western women. Family is a strong unit in Indian society and the sanctity of marriage is accepted in principle by the majority of Indian women. Welfare of the family is the uppermost ideal for a woman who has willingly effaced her 'self' in larger interests. It is necessary to consider the views of Madhu Kishwar on the differences between Indian and Western feminism. In her essay "A horror of isms: Why I do not call myself a feminist" she says that Western feminism is an offshoot of individualism and liberalism:

> In India most of us find it difficult to tune in to the extreme individualism that comes to us through feminism. For instance, most women here are unwilling to assert their rights in a way that estranges them not just from their family but also from their larger kinship group as community. They want to ensure that their rights are respected and acknowledged by their family and prefer to avoid asserting their rights in a way that isolates them from those they consider their own. This need not be interpreted as a sign of mental slavery to social opinion. Rather it is an indication that for many of us life is a poor thing if our freedom inevitably cuts us off from our interdependence with others. In our culture both men and women are taught to value the interests of our families and not make our lives revolve around individual self-interest. (272-3)

Though Western feminism is different from Indian feminism on conceptual basis nevertheless its impact is felt in India. Women dare to question the acts of injustice and oppression perpetrated on them and their fellow beings. Gender-based discrimination, social oppression and tyranny make women interrogate the past to find solutions to the present. The ideal role models in the ancient epics and puranas have inspired many a woman and they have become archetypes. The present change in the perspective makes women reassess the archetypal figures such as Sita, Savitri, Kunti and Gandhari. The lives of the ideal wives and ideal mothers make them rethink of the values of such a self-effacing womanhood. Sita's Agnipariksha is interpreted in terms of male-chauvinism and the need to protect against such a test of chastity is emphasized by the champions of women's cause.

Archetypes have been at the centre of racial consciousness. J.A. Cuddon in *A Dictionary of Literary Terms* defines an archetype as follows:

> a basic model from which copies are made, therefore a prototype. In general terms, the abstract idea of a class of things which represents the most typical and essential characteristics shared by the class thus a paradigm of exemplar . . . certain character or personality types have become established as more or less archetypal. (55-56)

Archetypes derive their significance from myths and legends which are rooted in a specific culture. Edward Quin's definition of the term myth in *A Dictionary of Literary and Thematic Terms* brings out the link between the two. He says that the myths are basically stories:

> stories belonging to a specific culture recounting supernatural or paradoxical events design to reflect the cultures' view of the world. Despite their seemingly endless variety, myths tend to have underlying consistency of action, theme and character. He says that a myth stands at the magnetic centre where several disciplines such as anthropology, psychology and philosophy converge. (207)

Indian sages and seers have fathomed the depth of the human psyche and by doing so they have delineated several character types which in the western system of epistemology could be called the archetype. Vedic and Upanishadic seers of India seem to have been of the opinion that poetic insight alone enables one to acquire wisdom with which life as it manifests itself can be understood. The poet, says the *Isavasyopanishad*, is self-born (*Swayambhu*), has absolute control over his mind and reveals things as they are (Yatha-tathyatah arthan vidadhati sasvatibhyah samabhyahi [8]) Responding to this sages as well as the poets in ancient India, tried to grasp the fundamentals of life in their infinite variety and projected them on to the mind of posterity. They seem to have made a deep study of each type of character (with reference to its characteristics). Thus one finds in the *Mahabharata*, the hero, the villain, the sage, the king, the eminent, the low and so on all marking a long list of characters who appear again and again evolving as they do along with the evolution of life.

It is the portrayal of characters of this kind especially in the *Mahabharata* and the *Ramayana* that is responsible for their being identified with the members of every family in India. Thus there is always a Shakuni who is responsible for the destruction of an entire family as there is always a Karna who is charity incarnate; and Krishna as a baby is present in every family from Kanyakumari to Kashmir. Therefore Vyasa and Valmiki can be said to have created characters who can in modern critical parlance be described as eternal archetypes.

The three novels taken up for study, not only reinterpret the characters but also interrogate the values signified by the archetypes. In *Parva* Gandhari the archetype of an ideal wife is recast in the modern social context and made to express her inner anguish arising out of being married to a blind king. Kunti also has nothing but contempt for her impotent husband.

Kunti and Draupadi in the same novel are also portrayed as miserable women who had unhappy marriages. Pratibha Ray's Yajnaseni reminds the reader of Bharathi's new woman who takes up the cause of justice and equality for women in the society. It is appropriate to quote Chellappan's views on Indian archetypes. In "Archetypes in Indian Literature" he says that the myths and legends have shaped and formed from the mind and imagination of our people all over the land. "But they were not simply vehicles of conscious meaning and they have acquired new areas of meaning from time to time and in different places. They are answers to the needs of deepest layers of the collective mind of India and also the metaliterature or the common code of the entire country" (74).

In the *Mahabharata* Karna's birth is traced to mythic origins. Kunti's boon from the sage Durvasa to beget children by reciting certain mantras is distorted by Bhyrappa in *Parva.* The episode is recast from a rational point of view and the myth is viewed in terms of human experience bereft of all supernatural quality about it. Joseph Campbell in *The Hero with a Thousand Faces* refers to folk stories of virgin motherhood and cites the example of the Buddha descending from heaven to his mother's womb in the shape of milk-white elephant. He says, "Any leaf accidentally swallowed, any nut, or even the breath of a breeze, may be enough to fertilize the ready womb. The procreating power is everywhere. And according to the whim or destiny of the hour either a hero, savior or a world annihilating demon may be conceived—one can never know" (311-20).

The life of Karna in the epic is an illustration of the later-day-theories of myth regarding the major motifs of the typical life of the hero as identified by Campbell: "Virgin birth, and quest for the father, ordeal, and atonement with the father, the assumption and coronation of the virgin mother and finally, the heavenly triumph of the true sons while the pretenders are heated hot" (312). The technique of demythologizing such episodes to throw light on the contemporary issues is discussed in the chapter on *Parva*. Even though individual writer's treatment of ancient myth sometimes leads to distortion, the myths cannot be totally destroyed as they are at the centre of racial consciousness. In the twentieth century, Jung postulated the theory of the Collective Unconscious. The collective unconscious is manifested in the recurrence of certain myths and images in literature. In "Psychology and Literature," he says that the poet interprets the contents of the collective unconscious.

> The psychological mode deals with the materials drawn from the realm of human consciousness with emotional shocks, the experience of passion and the crises of human destiny in general—all of which go to make up the conscious life of man and his feeling life in particular. This material is psychically assimilated by the poet, raised from the commonplace to the level of poetic experience and given an expression which forces the reader to greater clarity and depth of human insight by bringing fully into his consciousness what he ordinarily evades and overlooks or senses only with a feeling of dull discomfort. The poet's work is an interpretation and illumination of the contents of consciousness of the ineluctable experiences of human life with its eternally recurrent sorrow and joy. (Lodge 177)

The myth is of critical importance in literary works. Northrop Frye in "The Archetypes of Literature" says that "the myth is the central informing power that gives archetypal significance to the ritual and archetypal narrative to the oracle. Hence, the myth is the archetype, though it might be convenient to say myth only when referring to narrative and archetype when speaking of significance" (Lodge 429).

The literary artist's handling of the myth necessitates a serious study of the cultural history of the nation. Cassirer in his theory of myths points out that 'myth lays the basis for nationhood. It is behind the feeling of nationality and gives it its force' (Strenski 16). He finds it inconceivable that a nation should exist without mythology. Any attempt to distort the myth results in either the resurgence of the myth or the creation of yet another myth. In *Parva* Narakasura is portrayed as a highway robber who was killed by Krishna; Bhishma's mother Ganga is depicted as a member of the hill-tribes who belong to a matriarchal society where children are the property of the mother. Ganga's disposing of her seven children born to Shantanu is viewed as the prerogative of the mother belonging to that society. In place of the ancient myth of the Vasus who stole the cow of a sage doomed to undergo penance in the earth as Ganga's children, Bhyrappa has introduced a new myth.

There are a few instances in the novel which prove that myths cannot be successfully dispensed with. The archetypal approach to literature combines in itself the formalistic, sociological, anthropological, psychological and historical methods. Wilbur Scott in *Five Approaches of Literary Criticism* observes that the archetypal approach is "historical in its investigation of a cultural or social past, but nonhistorical in its demonstration of literature's timeless value, independent of particular period" (247).

What Scott says of the study of myths is true of the epic, as the study of epic in any nation is necessarily a study of its history. According to du Bois Page, "it is a representation in mixed narration of significant events in the past of a community" (1). Whereas history deals with the particular, the epic deals with the universal. Analyzing the relation between history and the epic, Page says, "in the epic poem there is an intersection between the fictive life of an individual and a vision of a larger history. Thus the lives of individuals with the destiny of the community are fitted into a larger pattern of time." He analyzes the art of historiography.

> History cannot of course be a pure 'real' account of what has happened—the telling of significant events in a community's past required selection and shaping. Time passes second by second; the historian arranges a version of an account of times passing which interprets events, attributes causation to various factors, foregrounds certain characters in the infinitely varied and chaotic flow of time. His interpretation of the past projects a shape for the future as well. (2)

The interconnections between history and the epic or literature in general are reinforced by the New Historicists. The writers who fictionalize the epic are, in fact, dealing with a complex material encompassing a fusion of history and fiction. Inevitably the process involves selection, omission and shaping of events and character. Tharoor not only deals with the history of the epic society but also with the history of a specific period, that is, the history of modern India. The novelist seems to have comprehended the assumptions of the New historicists. The assumptions are summed up by Raman Selden precisely and concisely in his *A Reader's Guide to Contemporary Literary Theory*, as follows:

> There are two meanings of the word 'history' (a) the events of the past and (b) telling a story about the events of the past. Poststructuralist thought makes it clear that history is always 'narrated' and that therefore the first sense is untenable. The past can never be available to us in pure form, but always in the form of representations. (105)

In the context of history being viewed as a narrative, in the form of representations Tharoor's questions in the novel regarding the relative significance of the story are relevant: "But to which story shall we return? Shall I tell of Karna's dramatic rise to national importance through his dominance of the Muslim Group? Shall I speak, instead, of Gangaji or of Dhritarashtra or should I turn instead to Pandu" (165). History cannot present the absolutes. Tharoor asks, "is it permissible to modify the truth with a possessive pronoun? At what point in the recollection of truth does wisdom cease to transcend knowledge? How much may one select, interpret and arrange the facts of the living past before truth is jeopardized by inaccuracy" (164).

These observations are further borne out by the contentions of the New Historicists.

> Historical periods are not unified entities. There is no single 'history' only discontinuous and contradictory 'histories.' There was no single Elizabethan world view. The idea of a uniform and harmonious culture is a myth imposed on history and propagated by the ruling classes in their own interests. Historians can no longer claim that their study of the past is detached and objective. We cannot transcend our own historical situation. The past is not something which confronts us as if it were a physical object, but is something we construct from already written texts of all kinds which we construct in line with our particular historical concerns (Selden 105).

A survey of the literary scene in the eighties and the nineties of twentieth century India shows that there has been a great revival of interest in the epics. To present an exhaustive survey of the re-renderings of the *Mahabharata* will be beyond the scope of the present study due to the encyclopedic nature of the growth of the epic. But it is necessary to present a brief review of a few of the significant works among the existing corpus.

As early as 1898 Romesh Chundar Dutt translated select verses of the *Mahabharata* with a motive to preserve the character and spirit of the original. According to R.C. Dutt, "the real facts of the war had been obliterated by age, legendary heroes had become the principal actors and as is invariably the case in India, the thread of a high moral purpose of the triumph of virtue and the subjugation of vice was woven into the fabric of the great epic" (151) R.C. Dutt views the epic as a tale of war and heroism and is impressed by the portraiture of the human character in its calm dignity of strength and repose. He calls the *Mahabharata* the greatest work of imagination that Asia has produced and finds the incidents of the epic very striking and significant. He regrets the unlimited expansion of the work (151). As a condensed version Dutt's *Mahabharata* serves as an introduction to the epic for the English reader but does not provide new insights into the epic.

C. Rajagopalachari's prose rendering of the *Mahabharata*, translated from a Tamil original into English in 1951, has remained till date the earliest source of inspiration for several writers who have no access to the Sanskrit original. Shashi Tharoor has acknowledged his indebtedness to C. Rajagopalachari for his first hand knowledge of the epic, which helped him in writing *The Great Indian Novel.* No other retelling of the *Mahabharata* has undergone as many, as thirty-editions, till date, as Rajaji's *Mahabharata.*

K.M. Munshi is the first Indian writer to produce an English rendering of the epic in prose, in seven volumes in 1962. He gave the tile *Krishnavatara* to the entire work though each volume has a separate subtitle. Munshi seems to have been enthralled by the divinity of Krishna. Munshi has faithfully adhered to the original though he has altered the chronological sequence of the episodes. The work seems to focus more on the glory of Krishna as divinity than on the conflict between the rival groups of the same dynasty to capture power. The prose style of Munshi is simple and direct.

In 1978, R.K. Narayan published his retelling of the epic of *Mahabharata.* Narayan recognizes the fact that the authorship is generally attributed to Vyasa. "while ninety-nine percent of our public would accept the name and venerate him without question as an immortal, inspired sage, research minded scholars have their own doubts and speculations" (8). He prefers to accept the traditional account of Vyasa as the author of *Mahabharata.* In his 'Introduction' R.K. Narayan states that his preference is the story although the epic is a treasure house of varied interests. He is struck by the well-defined characters who talk and act with robustness and zest (11). He claims that he has not omitted any of the significant episodes relevant to the destinies of the chief characters and has kept himself to the mainstream (12). Narayan's *Mahabharata* is yet another attempt at retelling the story by keeping to the original version of Vyasa. What is remarkable is the lucid style of Narayan that makes the work a delightful reading. The perspective that emerges from his retelling is in harmony with the traditional perspective.

Narayan's version ends with the coronation of Yudhishthir. In the epilogue R.K. Narayan states that "the writer of the epic has a disinclination to conclude a story. Just as all the action seems to be ending, one suddenly realizes that the last line is only the beginning of a new phase of the narrative, of fresh thoughts and experience. There is a reluctance to close the subject. This may be one way of creating a semblance of life itself, which is apparently endless. Nothing is ever really conclusive. More than a decade later, Tharoor echoes the opinion of R.K. Narayan when he refuses to conclude his story saying that stories never end and that he may have to retell the story again. R.K. Narayan's consummate skill of story-telling sustains the interest of the reader providing him with glimpses of the vitality of the timeless epic.

Summing up the literary activities in 1980s Pradip Bhattacharya says, in the 'introduction' to the Battle of Kurukshetra, that the eighties have been overwhelmingly the decade of the resurgence of myth. He finds in the post-independence India very few works to captivate the imagination of the reader. After K.M. Munshi's novels he finds only Buddhadeva Bose's reinterpretation of the episodes of the epic significant. According to him, Peter Brooks' dramatization of the epic on the International scene is a reassertion of the epic's universality. He finds the 80s marked by great creative endeavours:

> In the eighties, suddenly, the literary scene, as a matter of fact, the best seller market came throbbingly alive with a series of 12 novels in Hindi by Ram Kumar Bhramar. In Bengali came the spate of Dipak Chandra's and Kalkut's novels on both the *Ramayana* and the *Mahabharata* radically challenging our traditional points of view. In Oriya Pratibha Ray spoke for Draupadi in her novel of that name; in Marathi it was Shivaji Sawant writing Karna's autobiography the massive *Mrityunjaya*, in Kannada the tears, sweat, blood and mire of Kurukshetra were brought frighteningly alive by S.L. Bhyrappa's *Parva*. On the Bengali stage the agony of Draupadi husbandless though with five husbands was unforgettably brought home to entrance audiences in Shaoli Mitra's one-woman performance.

In 1987 Maggi Lidchi Grassi's *The Battle of Kurukshetra* appeared. She retells the story of the epic through the characters of Ashwathama and Arjuna. Maggi Lidchi Grassi portrays the conflict between the two families of the Kuru dynasty reaching the catastrophic depths at the battle of Kurukshetra. Through a probing of the psyche of the protagonists she brings out the conflict raging in the minds of Arjuna and Ashwathama. She views the inner anguish experienced by these characters as a kind of existential angst suffered by man in the twentieth century. She raises some very pertinent questions about Bhishma's silence during critical moments, such as Pandu's exile, Gandhari's blind-folding and Draupadi's disrobing. She seems to suggest that Bhishma's dharma is an outdated dharma as he was blinded by the splendour of his own renunciation.

As Pradip Bhattacharya suggests, Maggi Lidchi Grassi's unique quality lies in her ability to plumb these chinks in this superman's armour (20). It is his sense of failure that makes him advise Yudhishthir to follow a different dharma, the dharma of a king to rule and not abdicate the throne. By making Arjuna's quest, the quest of every individual at the threshold of the twenty-first century, she tries to relate the epic to the contemporary society.

The second volume of her trilogy is entitled *The Legs of the Tortoise* (1996). The significance of the title can be traced back to Bhishma's advice to Yudhishthira: "When desire comes, be as the tortoise; pull in your consciousness . . . nothing enslaves you more than desire." This volume vividly depicts Yuddha Parva, beginning with the conflict of Arjuna. Krishna's counselling of Arjuna which forms the content of *Bhagavad Gita* finds a poetic rendering in this novel. The tale of death and devastation is probed into with psychological insights. Grassi asserts that the end of the war marks the beginning of a new era when victors avoid celebration of their triumphs; but rather undergo a sort of spiritual transformation. Yudhishthir in the novel says, "After victory there are celebrations; today there is no victory. We are the sons of uncle Dhritarashtra mourning his sons, our brothers. Our wounds are green; it is a time for forgiveness and healing" (223).

Arjuna prepared himself to perform the Ashwamedha. But it will be different from the traditional Ashwameda. The novelist gives a new interpretation to the Yajna. "The Ashwameda is the way devised by man and blessed by gods to bring all our countries under one Emperor. It brings to all, wealth and stability. Gods shower down their blessings on a peaceful land. In times gone past the sacred horse was followed by an army and when it was opposed blood spilled over the issue (227). Yudhishthir is in no mood to rejoice over his victory as it leaves him with a sense of disillusionment; "Arjuna, I feel that the gods have taken those they chose. We are the Prasad nobody wants" (235). The aftermath of war is marked by a strong call for peace. "The earth wants peace" she said. "The earth has drunk the sacrifice of blood. She needs no more. She cannot take more blood" (318). Grassi has conceptualized peace as the outcome of the conquest of the self, an inner battle fought by the individual.

Shivaji Sawant's *Mrityunjaya*, published in 1989, translated from the Marathi original into English by P. Lal, is yet another recreation of *Mahabharata* from Karna's point of view. The novel is an autobiography of Karna projecting him as a tragic hero, a victim of the circumstances. Sawant attempts to probe the inner psyche of Karna by experimenting with narrative techniques. The novel contains nine books in first person narrative alternatingly given to Karna, Kunthi, Duryodhana, Shon his brother, Vrishali his wife and Krishna. His life is viewed in terms of his relationship with his mother, his brother, his wife and his friend. All the acts of heroism were inspired by the motifs of love, friendship and gratitude. Karna, rising from death to address the readers of the twentieth century, reveals the relevance of his life to the contemporary society. He reviews his entire life as a life of alienation marked by a quest for identity which in turn is a quest for the meaning of life itself.

Sawant gives the reader a poetic rendering of the epic, with evocative images. The images of cuckoo—kokila, the chariot meant to be drawn by six horses, with only five horses yoked to it, are a few examples of the poetic treatment of Karna's predicament. Karna expresses his anguish at being derided as the charioteer's son. There are a few deviations from Vyasa's epic; for example it is not Bhishma who arranges the marriage of Madri to Pandu but Pandu himself brings Madri home returning from his conquests. Karna's wife Vrishali emerges as a typical self-effacing Indian wife who commits Sati for an eternal union with her husband. The novelist does not seem to interrogate the values of an obsolete system which encourages women to practise 'Sati.' But he vehemently opposes any kind of discrimination based on caste/ community by projecting Karna as a victim of social ostracism.

Sawant modifies Vyasa's epic to suit his own purpose. Vrishali and Supriya the wives of Karna are all his poetic creations. He omits those episodes in which Karna becomes the loser, as seen in the episode of Drona's disciples attacking Panchala. Sawant selects those incidents which enhance the heroic image of Karna. In his zest to portray Karna as the beloved of all, Sawant makes even Draupadi yearn to become Karna's wife, which is inconsistent with the portrayal of Vyasa's Draupadi. In the game of dice Sawant's Karna is torn between his eagerness to rush to her rescue and his burning revenge for her disdain during her Swayamwara.

Sawant gives no conclusions to the quest of Karna. Pradip Bhattacharya in P. Lal's *Vyasa's Mahabharata: Creative Insights* says, "that uncertainty, that refusal of Sawant to provide the final answer resolving the multiple riddles faced by us in and through the persona of Karna, is precisely the feature which lifts their work far above the run of the mill best seller" (81)

In 1992 appeared M.M. Thakur's *Thus Spake Bhishma*. The novel is a significant contribution to the *Mahabharata* literature as the point of view changes, in this work in English. Novelists in the nineties have chosen to re-render the epic from the point of view of a major character. The Pitamaha of the epic, Bhishma is at the centre of the narrative in the first person. On his death-bed of arrows, Bhishma recalls the entire story of the epic. His reminiscences are also a simultaneous reassessment of his involvement in the dynastic rule of the Kuru family. In the very beginning Bhishma divests himself of the legendary glory of being greeted by showers of heavenly flowers when he took the vow of celibacy. He says, 'I must admit that I neither saw nor heard anything of the sort' (18).

The demythologising trend is perceptible throughout the narrative. Bhishma expresses his regrets over his acts of injustice to many a woman in the story and tries to wipe out any trace of heroism surrounding these acts. Referring to the wrong done to Amba, he says, "considering what my action or lack of it did to her life, what Shikhandin did to me was perfectly just. Indeed, if I owe my final freedom to anyone apart from Krishna, I owe it to Amba turned Shikhandin" (30).

There are some minor deviations from Vyasa's epic such as Shakuni arranging more Dandharis from his country for Dhritarashtra to have children outnumbering Pandu's, Draupadi spending a month with each of her husbands for practical convenience. Thakur's Bhishma dismisses the episode of Duryodhana poisoning Bhim's food or pushing him into the river as mere concocted stories. He seems to project Duryodhana as not so malicious as he is traditionally believed to be. He expresses his sympathy for Duryodhana when he was reported to be ridiculed by the woman of the House-of-All at Indraprastha.

It is significant point to note that Thakur's Bhishma admits to "shirking the duty of judging between right and wrong leaving it all to the person concerned, Yudhishthira himself, when Draupadi raised a question of propriety in the Kuru Sabha. After the experience of war Bhishma says that he has woken up to the "utter folly of the life that I have lived out, life that has passed so irretrievably beyond my control that even to regret it would be to add one more act of folly I have already let loose upon my time" (175). The novel presents an altogether new perspective to the epic by making Bhishma remorse stricken and views his life in retrospection as a miserable failure.

Vyasa's epic itself contains hints that give scope for such interpretations. For instance, his silence in the Kuru-Sabha, when Draupadi was disrobed by Dushasana, has puzzled many a reader. Amba's self-immolation is also viewed generally as the outcome of Bhishma's hasty action of carrying off the princesses of Kashi, misleading them into the belief that he was carrying them off for himself. The princesses were left to wonder whether he was going to break the vow of celibacy. The epic raises several such issues of morality.

M.T. Vasudevan Nair's *Second Turn* was first published in English in 1997. Though the original Malayalam version came out as early as 1977 the translation of the novel into English by K. Ravindranath came out twenty years later. The author has not altered the framework of the stories put together by Vyasa but claims that he has creatively exploited the silences in the original. The story is narrated in the first person from Bhima's point of view. According to the novelist Vyasa indicates that Yudhishthira is Vidura's son when Dhritarashtra mourns the latter's death. Such instances of Vyasa leaving significant pauses give ample scope to the reader to interpret the silences. In the epic Bhima is known for his gluttony, physical strength and courage to subdue his enemies. The epic tradition never endows him with a mind of his own but stresses his physicality.

V.C. Harris in his Introduction to the novel says: "To wrest this huge mass of body of the epic tradition endowing him with a raging mind and a tormented spirit and ultimately reading the whole of *Mahabharata* through this angle of vision—this is no mean achievement" (x). Bhima emerges as the only caring husband of Draupadi, with tremendous amount of love and loyalty. It is he who honours every little whim and fancy of Draupadi and remains her protector till the end; it is he who comes to her rescue when Jayadradh tries to abduct her or when Kichaka desires her. It is he who turns back to save her when she falls at the foot of the mount Meru when the Pandavas went on their last journey to heaven. Unlike the other Pandavas, Bhim expresses his sympathy for Karna when the latter is humiliated for his low descent.

Gandhari is portrayed as a wronged woman who comes to know of Dhritarashtra's blindness only at the time of her wedding. Duryodhana seems to question the genuineness of Pandavas' Kuru-lineage. Ekalavya's thumb is cut off by someone when he is asleep. These are a few instances of the novelist's attempts at recasting the events and interpretation of characters. V.C. Harris commends the artistic strategies.

> The re-reading / rewriting of the *Mahabharata* also involves a demythification of the epic, a process by which the novel successfully steers clear of all kinds of spiritualist traps that contemporary revisitations of the past often fall into. Indeed the text is so clearly conscious of its own status that at times one hears Bhima talking about the possible ways in which he would be read and talked about by posterity—a narrative/ interpretive strategy that helps the text keep a firm hold on its own little ironies and subversive potential. (xii)

Apart from these re-renderings of the epic in the mode of fiction there are numerous poems, plays and short stories based on select episodes from the *Mahabharata.* Most of these works are compiled and edited by P. Lal in two separate volumes, entitled *Vyasa's Mahabharata: Creative Insights.* The first volume was published by the Writers Workshop in 1992 and the second volume in 1997. P. Lal says in his Preface to the first volume, "To take from the air a live tradition. . . . That is what I had in mind when I planned this anthology." His rhetoric assets the multiplicity of messages in the *Mahabharata* inspiring a humble secondary tribe of adapters, reviewers and transcreators. P. Lal's two volumes include critiques and book reviews too.

In 1996 Pavan K. Varma published his *Yudhishtir and Draupadi.* It is a poetic narrative based on a particular episode of Yudhishtir facing the challenges from Yaksha of the poisoned tank. The narrative brings out the wisdom and diplomacy of Yudhishtir in handling a difficult situation and becomes a short commentary on the nature of life. The episode also throws light on the complex relationship between Yudhishtir and Draupadi since Draupadi is said to have loved more than any other Pandava. The author has used the episode to comment on the nature of man-woman relationship. Pavan K. Varma's work is an instance of creative exploitation of even a small episode from the epic.

A Gujarati novel entitled *Kurukshetra*, written by Manubhai Pancholi Darshak, needs a special mention in this study. The novel has been translated into Hindi and English but not yet published in English. The novel has won the Saraswati Samaan Award for the year 1997. This novel gives an entirely new perspective to the story of the *Mahabharata* by making the central issue a conflict between the races, the Aryans and the Naagas. The ethnic strife is woven around the tale of love between Tapati and Takshaka. Tapati is the Daughter of sage Dhaumya, the family priest of the Pandavas and Takshaka is the son of a Naaga King Chitraratha. The Naagas have a genuine grouse against the Pandavas for burning the forests of Khandavaprastha during their exile. Takshaka's mother Chintamani and her brother Vasuki, the ashramites of

Dhaumya, advocate unity between the Aryans and the Naagas and they face counter moves from Chitraratha.

The racial conflict is foregrounded in the novel, and all the other events leading to the battle of Kurukshetra are marginalized. The latter part of the novel gives a vivid account of the war and the involvement of Tapati and Takshaka in the opposite campaigns. Tapati's efforts at retrieving the uninhabited land of Khandavavana from the Pandavas to the Naagas signify the move towards reconciliation and amity between the two races. All the tangles complicating the tender tale of love between Tapati and Takshaka are resolved by Bhishma's statement, "My stepmother was the daughter of a fisherman, a Matsyakanya in her youth. She became Satyavatee at a later stage. All the social stratifications are merely a part of administrative convenience so that society could function properly. The social laws are not divine ones. They cannot become non-trespassable" (217).

The unpublished novel in English has great relevance for the contemporary political situation in India, where the Naagas, the Bodos and various tribals demand a recognition of separate state for them. *Darshak* seems to focus on the mini-Kurukshetras in the lives of different races seeking a separate identity for themselves and the basic right to human dignity in contemporary India.

M.S. Rao's *The Great Stories Retold: Ramayana and Mahabharata* published in 2000 by Horseshoe publication, UK, is the latest retelling of the *Mahabharata.* Like Tharoor, M.S. Rao also adopts an irreverent tone in the narrative. But Tharoor's irreverent tone helps him in his political satire whereas Rao's irreverence is only a device to present the story from the point of view of modern youth. The use of initials as D or DP, or AT is a feature of the colloquial idiom of the modern times. Rao has dealt with certain issues of moral importance in his retelling and the work has been well commenced for his attempt to explain every nuance and doubt with care and diligence. The *Mahabharata* is a text that every age claims for itself and the process of revisioning and rediscovery continues even today and will continue into the future.

Alongside the creative endeavours there are also critical works and commentaries on the *Mahabharata.* P. Lal's two volumes entitled *Vyasa's Mahabharata: Creative Insights* contain poems, plays, short stories, critiques and book reviews on the recreations of the *Mahabharata*. Shashi Tharoor's "The Relevance of the *Mahabharata* in Today's India," in Lal's first volume, spells out the intention of Tharoor to write a political satire using the framework of the epic. *The Mahabharata Revisited* is a Sahitya Akademi publication of the papers presented at the International Conference on the *Mahabharata* at New Delhi (1987). This volume contains S.L. Bhyrappa's "The *Mahabharata*: My Attempt at Recreation" in which the novelist expresses the determination to limit the epic to a strict human possibility and view it from the twentieth century perspective.

The critical reviews of the primary texts shown are only a few, since they are recent works by promising contemporary writers. There is no full length study available on any of the primary texts chosen. The secondary sources are limited to a few critical essays, journal articles and formal interviews given by the novelists to reputed journals.

Among the significant pieces, Pratibha Ray's interview given to Ranavir Ranga in *Indian Literature* reveals her commitment to the oppressed group that includes the women and the tribals. In conversation with Sue Dicman, Ray makes it clear that the feminist issues in her works are concerned with human rights.

In the following chapters the significant issues dealt with in the primary texts are discussed. In the second chapter, issues relating to revisioning of history by Tharoor in *The Great Indian Novel* are analyzed. The next chapter examines the predicament of women and the oppressed group as portrayed by Pratibha Ray in *Yajnaseni*. The fourth chapter is a study of the socio-cultural issues implicit in Bhyrappa's *Parva*. The concluding chapter discusses the common ideology behind the re-renderings of the epic and the contemporary relevance of the epic.

Chapter II

The Politics of History: Shashi Tharoor's *The Great Indian Novel*

Shashi Tharoor's *The Great Indian Novel* is an attempt at fictionalizing the epic to expound the contemporary relevance of the *Mahabharata*. Tharoor says, in "The Relevance of the *Mahabharata* in Today's India," that in considering the *Mahabharata* a suitable vehicle for an attempt to retell the political history of twentieth century India albeit—through a fictional recasting of its events, episodes and characters—I have, after all, already made an unabashed case for its contemporary relevance" (La 1:339).

While fictionalizing the epic, the novelist resorts to selection, omission, addition, rearrangement reinterpretation and recasting of events from Vyasa's epic. The epic is used as a framework to reassess the political history of modern India. In the process the classical epic is reassessed and interpreted from the twentieth century perspective. Ayyappa Panikar remarks, "The Great Indian Novel is a literary tour-de-force undermining the age-old Indian complacency displayed in accepting everything ancient and anything foreign" (13).

According to Tharoor, 'to retell the *Mahabharata* is to recall the kind of stories a society tells about itself" (Lal 1:346) and the story chosen is about the historical events of modern India and the novel becomes "a song of Modern India" in prose. Ved Vyas or VV in short is the narrator and his aim is spelt out in the beginning of the novel itself. "In my epic I shall tell of the past, present and future especially of existence and passing of efflorescence and decay, of death and re-birth of what is, of what was and what should have been" (18).

Alok Prasad in '(Un) Intentionally (Un) Familiar' says that "in retelling a two thousand year-old tale set in contemporary India Shashi Tharoor manages to convey a sense of continuity and change which is so much a part of the Indian Kaleidoscope" (41). V.V. of Tharoor functions like Tiresias of Eliot transcending time and space, narrating the political history of modern India.

Tharoor deliberately adopts an irreverent tone while describing the eccentric traits of a particular character or commenting on certain events. The novelist feels a certain degree of irreverence to be essential in the telling. "I took heart from the conviction that irreverence in the Indian tradition is not sacrilege; as the *Mahabharata* amply demonstrates, the epics themselves ascribe human qualities, imperfection, base motives, and feet of clay even in the gods" (Lal 1:347). The irreverent tone serves the purpose of satirizing the political history of India and it does not violate the sanctity of the epic.

The novelist adopts various narrative strategies and stylistic devices to facilitate the superimposition of the structure of the epic on the political history of India. The use of parallelism and contrast alternating between the modes of prose and verse, resorting to dream sequence and direct reporting are some of the narrative techniques adopted by Tharoor. Besides, there are deviations from the epic, sometimes amounting to distortions and deliberate recasting of events due to compulsions of artistic necessity. Other stylistic devices include use of irony, parody and an inextricable combination of satire and humour.

Tharoor identifies conflict and confrontation as the common thematic link between the epic and history. Commenting on the thematic analogy M.K. Chaudhuri in *Recent Indian Fiction* observes: "What the Great Indian Novel fundamentally tries to underline is the continuance of the historical process, the pastness of the present and the presentness of the past" (108). He finds T.S. Eliot's oft quoted lines in *Burnt Norton*—Time present and time past / Are both perhaps contained in time future / And time future contained in time past"—modified in Ved Vyasa's words: "We are all living in an eternal present in which what was and what will be is contained in what is" (108). He further adds that the use of parallelism as an effective strategy in the novel serves to underline the truth, history is Kurukshetra. In the epic conflict is purely an internal one a sort of fraternal feud between the members of the same Kuru dynasty, the Pandavas and the Kauravas. But in the novel which depicts the history of modern India the conflict is at two levels: the major external conflict between Indian Nationalists and the British Imperialists, that is, between the colonizer and the colonized and an internal conflict between the Hindus and Muslims which led to the partition of India.

Indian nationalists are the members of the Kaurava party who spearheaded the revolt against the British. The Pandavas in the novel are the dissident members of the Kaurava Party led by Pandu (Bose) who urged the adoption of a harder line against the British (121). The British, on the other hand, are represented by Sir Richard the Resident, a special representative of the British, his assistants, Ronny Heaslop, Colonel Rudyard (Gen. Dyre), the Viceroy Lord Drewpad (Lord Mountbatten) and his wife Lady Georgina Drewpad. Among the British only Lord Mountbatten is compared to Dhrupad of the epic and no other parallels from the epic are drawn to represent the British.

Tharoor's novel exhibits the characteristics of postmodernistic historiographic metafiction if one attempts a careful examination of all the strategies used by the novelist. The significant aspects of the form include an interrogation of traditional history—social, political and cultural—rendering of multiple meanings, denial of absolute truth, an element of indeterminacy, self-reflexivity, intertextuality, parody, subversion and rejection of closure or closed ending. Many of these features evident in *The Great Indian Novel* are worth a serious study.

Tharoor draws parallels between the epic and history in terms of both characters and events. There is a broad matching of characters between the epic and history. He juxtaposes the literary epic with history without privileging the former text. The two texts operate as inter-texts running parallel to each other mutually interrogating and informing each other. The striking parallels are Gangaji—Gandhiji, Dhritarashtra—Nehru, Pandu—Subhash Chandra Bose, Vidur—Patel / Sri Aurobindo Ghose, Drona—Jayaprakash

Narayan, Kanika—Krishna Menon, Drupad—Lord Mountbatten, Dushasana—R.K. Dhawan, Shakuni—Siddharth Shankar Ray, Yudhishtir—Moraraji Desai, Draupadi—Draupadi Mokrasi, Ekalavya—V.V. Giri, Amba—Shikhandin—Godse and so on.

Tharoor throws broad hints and clues to the reader to identify the parallels. He uses biographical details, ironic exaggeration of the peculiar traits of the characters, homophonic words or a mere play on words to suggest the parallels, for example, Manimir for Kashmir, Gelabi Desh for Bangladesh, Jinnah for Karna. The Congress party is portrayed as the Kaurava party. Just as the epic is held in high esteem, the Congress party has also been respected and appreciated for several decades for its contribution to the winning of Independence for India. To portray the Congressmen as Kauravas is a strategy that simultaneously highlights and subverts the image of Congressmen. The sacrifice and involvement in the struggle for Indian Independence have elevated them to the rank of heroes and martyrs. But the inherent weaknesses and failures of the Congress Party expose them as Kauravas who brought about the decadence of the country. The reader's attention is drawn to the state of decay of the Congress party.

It is important to recognize the parallelism in characters before a detailed study of the novel is attempted. Both the Gangaji of the novel and the Gandhiji of history have striven hard to protect the integrity of the country against annexation by foreign powers. Both were respected as Pitamaha / Father of the Nation by the people. Strangely enough both took upon themselves the responsibility of protecting the throne without the authority to rule. The terrible vow of celibacy, a reputation for triumph without resorting to violence, an illimitable simplicity are the other common character traits between Gangaji and Gandhiji. After highlighting the glory of both Gangaji and Gandhiji, Tharoor subverts the images of these great men by drawing the attention of the reader to the failures of the two.

Bhishma of the epic was a sad witness to the division of the country into Hastinapur and Khandavaprastha. His sacrifice went in vain as he failed to avert the catastrophe of war and the resultant disintegration. The Pitamaha of modern India also could not avert the disaster of partition. He struggled in vain to mediate between the Hindus and the Muslims. Conflict within the party threatened the unity of the country. The conflict between the extremists and the moderates in the party and the conflict between the leaders of the Hindu and Muslim communities were aggravated by the British policy of divide and rule.

Gandhi even suggested premiership to M.A. Jinnah to avert the disaster of partition. But it was resented by Nehru. Tharoor's daring portrayal of the failures of Gandhi is an instance of a change in the perspective of the contemporary society. Gandhi, it must be admitted, was not an infallible superhuman being; he has indeed, committed several blunders. One such blunder was his promoting the political fortunes of Nehru at the cost of diminishing the greatness of Subhash Chandra Bose. Tharoor says, "it was Pandu who took the party banners into the most remote villages while Dhritarashtra toured the lecture halls and the meeting rooms of Urban India" (111). Gandhiji anointed Dhritarashtra "his successor" (121).

Tharoor does not ignore the eccentricities of the characters while describing them. Gandhiji's thin-rimmed glasses that gave him the look of a startled owl (35), his obsession with enema (the British call him Public Enema Number one), his renunciation of sex, all this noise about "equality and toilet cleaning" are some of his eccentricities exposed by the novelist. The element of parody is obvious in, "my vow has never been so sorely tested but I won't give in to untruth for any reason" followed by the authorial voice "he tried not to sound pompous while saying this and nearly succeeded" (31).

It is not difficult to identify the Dhritarashtra of the novel as Jawaharlal Nehru since the novelist refers to his early education at Eton and Cambridge. Blindness is a point of analogy between the Dhritarashtra of the epic and the Nehru of history. There are frequent references to his blindness.

Dhritarashtra was a fine-looking young fellow, slim, of aquiline nose and aristocratic bearing. His blindness was, of course, a severe handicap, but he learned to act as if it did not matter (41). "Dhritarashtra revelled in optical illusions." (84). Dhritarashtra had the blind man's gift of seeing the world not as it was but as he wanted it to be" (85).

The analogy between Nehru and Dhritarashtra makes the reader revise his opinion of both. The Dhritarashtra of the epic would have proved himself an ideal king if he had not been motivated by selfishness and excessive love for his son. In fact, many versions of the epic portray him as fair-minded and sensible in the beginning but turned out to be selfish by gradually yielding to the temptations of retaining the throne for his son due to the influences of his Minister Kanika and the evil influence of Shakuni on his son. In Vyasa's epic he offers the throne to his brother Pandu without a sense of bitterness or resentment. He emerges as a kind-hearted father-in-law to Draupadi. In the epic it is his generosity and sympathy for Draupadi that made him grant three boons to her to set her husbands free.

It is not so much the physical blindness of Dhritarashtra but his mental blindness that brought about the ruin of the Kauravas. Krishna Chaitanya commenting on the blindness of Dhritarashtra says, "while many have striven hard and succeeded in compensating such handicaps, he let his physical blindness grow into a mental unawareness of reality and an increasing distaste for squarely confronting the hard facts of life . . . forced into physical inaction, he let his mind too become apathetic" (45).

In Tharoor's novel, comparison of Nehru with Dhritarashtra serves to highlight Nehru's blind idealism and his excessive love for his daughter that weakened the country and the organization. Dhritarashtra is the unseeing visionary and Gangaji's favourite in the novel. T.N. Dhar in "Entering History through the Backdoor: Tharoor's *The Great Indian Novel*" says that "the novelist gives an extremely negative estimate of Nehru's abilities and role in the politics of pre-post independence India" (140). He is implicated in the nasty deal of partition. His bungling of the Kashmir issue and extreme shortsightedness in taking it to the United Nations, his wrong policies of industrialization ignoring the harsh realities of the basic needs of the poor, promoting non-alignment without assessing the country's strength to give it a meaningful credibility and at a personal level his amatory liaison with Edwina Mountbatten, neglect of his wife, cumulatively present a negative estimate of Nehru, as observed by Dhar:

> By concentrating solely on deficiencies in Nehru's person and policies, his vision touches the other extreme, and lacks the balance one finds in his portrait of Gandhi. If the earlier estimates of Nehru were fired by excesses of one kind, Tharoor's is characterized by excess of another kind. The only credit Nehru gets is that he was not guilty of meanness or villainy.

But Tharoor's portrayal is not too biased as he appreciates Nehru's merits, too, as evident in his upholding parliamentary democracy. "For all Dhritarashtra's sins and limitations that was one conviction he never betrayed . . . he constantly reaffirmed and encouraged the institution of parliamentary democracy in the country" (320).

R.K. Kaul expresses similar opinion in his review of the novel in *Indian Book Chronicle*. He says, "the writer goes out of the way to vilify the character and contribution of Nehru" (1). Tharoor deliberately indulges in ironic understatements and uses parody to shake the complacency of the reader. Perhaps, it is suggested that the blind veneration of the great leaders by the public has resulted in glossing over the weaknesses of these great leaders. P. Balaswamy says, "in the portrayal of Dhritarashtra Tharoor pours in enough subjectivity in true postmodernistic manner that robs away any offensiveness" (232). If the intent of the novelist is well-understood then the exaggeration does not hurt the sentiments of the reader. As Chaudhuri says, Tharoor uses parallelism as "a defamiliarizing technique for the purpose of modifying the usual perception of the political personalities and issues not only of the modern Indian but also those of the epic age" (113). Tharoor's portrayal of Gandhi and Nehru is also a reflection of the twentieth century mind which questions the blind veneration and accepts the imperfections of the great leaders, while in the past they were adoring them as infallible heroes. The great epic itself is a commentary on human fallibility and the use of parallel is an effective device to provide fresh insights into history and the epic.

While introducing Bose, Tharoor again makes a direct reference to his education and incidents in early life. Modern India's Pandu "insisted with more pride than judgment on pursuing his studies in India rather than English; he was expelled from one of the country's best colleges for striking a teacher, an Englishman who called the Indians dogs" (42). The details point to Subhash Chandra Bose who was expelled from the Presidency College, Calcutta, for striking Prof. Oaten who referred to the Indians in contemptuous terms. Using the same context, the novelist has a dig at the slavish altitude of some of the Indians who were keen on pleasing the British:

> Yes we Indians do have a number of dog-like characteristics, such as wagging out tails at white men carrying sticks and our bark is usually worse than our bite. . . . Pandu never lacked in strength or courage . . . he did take to wearing little roundish glasses that gave him the appearance of a Bengali teacher or a Japanese admiral. (42)

Tharoor draws a contrast between Nehru and Bose and makes his preference for Bose explicit. Such a review is a reflection of the sentiments of a majority of Indians today who believe that Bose was overshadowed and sidelined by Nehru. He was marginalized by both Nehru and Gandhi, according to the novelist. In Vyasa's epic Pandu was given the kingship as Dhritarashtra was blind. He proved his valour and heroism in military exploits, just as Pandu of modern India never lacked strength or courage. In the novel differences between Pandu and Dhritarashtra and between Pandu and Gangaji weakened the Kaurava party and set the divisive forces at work. Such differences are true of history but much less of the epic. Pandu felt that the masses were ignored by some of the educated leaders who appealed only to the urban population. During the presidential election (1939) he openly opposed Dhritarashtra and accounted his candidacy for the presidency of the Kaurava party. Dhritarashtra was shaken. Gangaji advised him to step down to avoid humiliating defeat. According to the narrator, Dhritarashtra was a shrewd politician who withdrew from the contest aiming at something higher, that is the post of the Prime Minister. Pandu was able to defeat the candidate (Dr. Pattabi Sitaramiah) who was the choice of Gangaji. Differences between Pandu and Dhritarashtra widened and Pandu at one stage resigned and quit the party. The comments of the narrator on the exile and death of Pandu record his anguish and sorrow; "Pandu's loss diminished us all" (191).

The obvious inference is true of both the epic and history. If the Pandu of the epic had survived he would have perpetuated the Kuru dynasty and would have ably averted the disastrous partition and disintegrations better than Bhishma whose struggles and sacrifice were in vain. Commenting on the contrast implied by the novelist, T.N. Dhar says, "the narrative suggests that Nehru gained influence in the party hierarchy and succeeded in controlling the reins of power in post-Independence India, because of the blessings of Gandhi. This is suggestively reinforced by Bhishma's continuance in the court of Dhritarashtra, even after he knew of the falsity of the Kauravas" (131). The separation between Pandu and Dhritarashtra, according to the narrator, was inevitable, "Pandu became impatient of Dhritarashtra's oratorical certitudes, his lofty convictions and vaulting ambition. Dhritarashtra, in turn, had little time for Pandu's atavistic traditionalism, his political earthiness, his pride in his wife's five boys" (112).

Tharoor doesn't draw a one-to-one correspondence between his parallels. Some characters are given double or multiple identities to suit the purpose of his political satire. Vidur Dharmaputra of the novel could be either Sri Aurobindo Ghose or Sardar Patel as is warranted by the context. The biographical details point to Sri Aurobindo Ghose: "In intellectual gifts and administrative ability he outshone his two brothers but knowing from the beginning that unlike them he had no claim on a kingly throne, he developed a sense of modesty and self-effacement that would enhance his effectiveness in his chosen profession. . . . Vidur topped the written examinations to the ICS" (42).

"That he served the State Department and had been a Union Minister" could point to Patel. But historically the trio Nehru—Patel—Bose, can be equated with the three brothers of the epic—Dhritarashtra, Pandu and Vidur. Dhritarashtra's minister in the epic, Kanika, becomes Kanika Menon in the novel. The obvious reference is to Krishna Menon who was a close aide of Nehru and served the Union Cabinet as Defence Minister during Nehru's tenure as Prime Minister. The parallel between Kanika and Krishna Menon is suggestive of the intrigue and equivocation making the counsel perpetually offered by Kanika to Dhritarashtra and the parallelism holds good for both the epic and history.

The Dhritarashtra—Nehru analogy also serves to focus on the relationship between Dhritarashtra and Gandhari. In the epic, Gandhari's blindfolding is an act of her devotion to her husband. Both in the epic and in history Gandhari emerges as a much neglected, suffering wife of Dhritarashtra. The Gandhari of the epic is the archetype of an ideal wife who silently suffered on account of her marriage to a blind man.

She remained 'a pativrata' till her death. Her image remains exemplary to the Indian women. The Gandhari of the novel is Kamala Nehru who was sadly neglected by her husband. Nehru was blind to her emotional and physical needs and devoted himself more to enhancing his public image than to discharging his duties as a responsible husband.

Referring to her death, Tharoor says, "I stepped soundlessly forward to where Gandhari lay, neglected in death as in life. Tenderly in a gesture that I could not explain, I crossed her palms across her chest. Then, ignored by her husband and daughter lost in mutual consolation, I eased the terrible bandage of her face" (217). In the epic Gandhari's death comes at the end when she walks to the forest fire along with her husband. It is the inevitable fact of history that compels Tharoor to show Gandhari dying much earlier, survived by her husband and daughter.

The Kunti Yadav of Tharoor is one of the characters whose identity is kept unmatched by any other character, or political personage of modern India. On the other hand, Kunti Yadav represents Mother India guarded by her sons, the Pandavas, who stand for the pillars of democracy. The Kunti of the novel stands for the diversified / composite culture of India in a state of political fragmentation. The narrator finds her ethnic beauty stained by the cultural invasion of the west:

> She was seated in the living room, half-smoked Turkish cigarettes overflowing from a nearby ashtray whose silver matched the tint of the hair at her temples. Her Benares saree, Bombay nails, Bangalore sandals and Bareilly bangles all advertised her fabled elegance, an elegance betrayed only by the stain at the corner of her eyes and by the quick darting puffs she took through her ivory cigarette holder. (265-66)

Kunti's identity as the wife of Pandu finds no parallel in history. The reference to diversified cultural aspects in the description of Kunti's elegance could be an allusion to her predicament of having to beget children through various gods as depicted in the epic, following the custom of Niyoga. Tharoor seems to satirise this custom when he refers to Kunti as 'the faithfully infidelious' wife of Pandu and Pandu in turn as 'the absentee landlord of Kunti's womb' (86).

Tharoor keeps to the epic of Vyasa while referring to Kunti as the unwed mother of Karna. "It seems, he went on, that Miss Yadav might have conducted a brief and unwisely liaison with a certain Hyperion Helios, a foreign visitor at her father's place" (44). The term Hyperion Helios is the Greek equivalent of Indian Sun-God who is supposed to have fathered Karna in Vyasa's epic. Her brief encounter with Hyperion Helios is referred to as her indiscretion in the past and errors of youth. It is a well known fact to any casual reader of the epic that Kunti suffered indignity and inner anguish on account of her status as the unwed mother of Karna. The narrator seems to exonerate her by calling it an act of indiscretion and errors of youth.

Tharoor draws a parallel between Karna and Jinnah and makes the identity obvious by calling him Mohammed Ali Karna. The narrator gives adequate biographical details about Mohammed Ali Karna. He refers to M.A. Karna's father as a man in a driver's uniform alluding to Karna's foster parent Adiratha, a charioteer by profession. He is considered to be an eminent leader. "Before long it began to be said that if there was an Indian of his generation born to shine and to lead it, it was clearly the illustrious Mohammed Ali Karna. . . . Karna had joined the Kaurava party upon his return from London to set up practice in Bombay as a barrister"

(136). Karna's learning and intelligence enhanced his qualities of leadership. The narrator adds that though Karna was known for his arrogance, his arrogance inspired respect rather than resentment.

He begins his political career by joining the Kaurava (Congress) party. Prema Nandakumar observes, "Vyasa's Radheya Karna and Tharoor's Mohammed Ali Karna run on identical parallel tracks, thanks to Tharoor's extravagant imagination" (22). Parallelism between Karna and Jinnah seems to convey the idea that both could have been ideal leaders to head the country but were defeated by origins.

While dealing with Dhritarashtra—Karna relationship, Tharoor has to deviate from the epic due to compulsions of history. Karna had to leave the Kaurava party as differences broke out between him and Dhritarashtra and Gangaji. In the epic Karna never left the Kauravas until his death. His differences with Gangaji are true of the epic too. There were several reasons for Karna of modern India to leave the Kaurava Party.

Mohammed Ali Karna decided to free himself from the hegemony of the Hindus. Tharoor comments that Karna was not much of a Muslim but he found Gangaji too much of a Hindu" (141). It is true that Jinnah was not a fanatic Muslim but was forced to join the Muslim group on account of his differences with Gandhi and Nehru: A "Kaurava party of prayer meetings and unselective eclecticism was not a party he would have cared to lead, let alone to remain a member of" (141). In Tharoor's novel Mohammed Ali Karna admits, "in the ordinary course I would have been reluctant to identify myself solely with one community. But I do not like the direction that the Kaurava movement is taking" (141). As a result he became the leader of a separate group which wanted "Independence without Hindu Nationalism" (147). Differences between M.A. Karna and Dhritarashtra are true of history but not of the epic. Tharoor's portrayal of Karna is in keeping with the popular tradition of viewing him as a tragic hero.

Prema Nandakumar says, "It is of the nature of the creative wand that makes heroes out of "villains." If Satan is the hero of Milton's' *Paradise Lost*, Karna is the most unforgettable tragic hero of Vyasa and has been favourite of the creative writers down the centuries" (25). She cites Uloor Parameswara Aiyar's *Karna Bhushanam* (Malayalam), B.S. Ramiah's *Therotti Manan* (Tamil), T.G.P. Kailasam's *Karna* or *The Brahmin's Curse* (English), Shivaji Sawant's *Mrityunjaya* (Marathi) and M. Raman's *Kama* (English) as examples of contemporary works that treat Karna as a tragic hero.

Karna-Jinnah parallelism is yet another instance of the need to reassess and reinterpret these characters in both the epic and history. The comparison provokes consideration of several probabilities. Both had the potential of excellence in valour and heroism. In the classical epic it was Karna who had several conquests to his credit and helped expand the empire of Hastinapur. If he had not been a victim of fate he would have kept up the integrity of the Kuru dynasty.

Jinnah too would have been an ideal leader in India if he had not been denied the importance due to him. Tharoor calls him the finest of Indians. Both were marginalized by the hostility of circumstances. If Karna's true identity as the eldest of the Pandavas had been revealed, he would have ascended the throne and the catastrophe of war and resultant disintegration would have been averted. The same argument could be applied to Jinnah. If Nehru had conceded the Premiership to Jinnah, probably the disaster of partition could have been averted.

The Duryodhani of the novel stands in comparison with the Duryodhana of the epic. The myth of Gandhari having a hundred sons is shared by Tharoor to suit the purpose of his art. He uses the framework of the classical epic chiefly to satirise the political history of modern India. Artistic necessity compels him to deviate from the classical epic and so he makes Gandhari give birth to a daughter Priya Duryodhani instead of a hundred sons. The change of gender is in line with the subverting strategy of the postmodernistic historiographic metafiction. R.K. Kaul remarks that in postmodern narratives, the author takes liberties with the historical facts and he alters the sequence of events. He says, "for example the game of dice is placed at the end of the story. The reader doesn't mind distortions such as Gandhari giving birth to one daughter (Priya Duryodhani) instead of hundred sons" (10).

Priya Duryodhani is described as having a high-pitched squeaky voice and lustrous eyes. In the novel she is one 'who never married' (335). Giving her the status of a single woman is also in keeping with the subverting strategy to portray her, as a hardened female who never wept except when her mother Gandhari died. This fictional twist enables the novelist to portray Indira Gandhi, satirically. The parallelism, serves to depict her as one who in her determination, obsession with power, wilfulness and ruthlessly autocratic style of functioning matches the hundred Kauravas of the epic, led by Duryodhana.

Kunti Yadav stands for Mother India and is not compared to any of the political personages of twentieth century India—Draupadi Mokrasi also represents Indian democracy. She is not equated with any of the historical figures of modern India. The art of fictionalizing gave Tharoor the freedom to portray the characters of the epic to suit the context. Hence, Draupadi of the epic stands for the ideal of Indian democracy. The name Draupadi Mokrasi is highly suggestive of democracy made a mockery and farce during the tenure of Indira Gandhi as Prime Minister. The birth of Indian democracy was not at the right time, according to Tharoor. It was born at the wrong time to parents of conflicting cultures. The squalling premature baby was born to Lady Georgina Drewpad and Dhritarashtra.

G.N. Devy strongly objects to the portrayal of Draupadi Mokrasi in Tharoor's novel. He says: "Tharoor has to go through such a circus of imagination in finding modern parallels to the epic characters. One example should suffice: Democracy is seen as a daughter of illicit love between Nehru and Edwina Mountbatten. She is named Draupadi Mokrasi. Is the idea amusing?" (32) Tharoor never intended one-to-one correlation between the parallels of history and the epic and hence the charges against lack of complete matching of parallels can be dismissed.

Tharoor's depiction of Draupadi Mokrasi is suggestive of more than one thing. It creates an impression that freedom was given to India when the country was least prepared for it. Tharoor remarks that Lord Mountbatten acted in indecent haste and granted India freedom at the wrong time. Conflicting forces of factionalism and imperialism made up the sacrificial fire out of which Draupadi Mokrasi was born and her birth is symbolic of the hybrid nature of Indian democracy. Tharoor does not fail to allude to the intimate friendship between Nehru and Edwina Mountbatten who are the parents of Draupadi Mokrasi.

If Draupadi Mokrasi was wedded to the Pandavas then, the identity of the Pandavas has to be comprehended in harmony with the relationship. It becomes evident that the Pandavas stand for the five pillars of democracy; Law and Justice, Army, Press (Fourth Estate), Indian Administrative service and Indian Foreign Service. Commenting on Draupadi's marriage to Arjun, M.K. Chaudhuri says, that the marriage is given a meaning by presenting it as a union of democracy and the voice of the people, whose medium is the press. The modern Arjuna is a journalist, a representative of the powers and weaknesses of the Indian press. "I thought of Arjuna," says Ved Vyasa, "with this paradoxical mixture of attributes as the spirit of the Indian people, to whom he so ably gave voice as a journalist" (320). Chaudhuri considers Arjuna's Pashupat Astra obtained from Shiva symbolic of the power of the press in a democracy (112). Only the eldest of the Pandavas, Yudhishthir, is given a double identity later in the novel as he is compared to Morarji Desai who succeeded Indira Gandhi as the Prime Minister.

Tharoor's choice of Duryodhani to represent Indira Gandhi serves to expose the unscrupulous means pursued by both the Duryodhana of the epic and his fictional counterpart in history to achieve their selfish ends. Shakuni of the epic stood by Duryodhana adding fuel to the fire of his ambition. Tharoor refers to Siddharth Shankar Ray as the counterpart of Shakuni who was the close confidant of Indira Gandhi offering unflinching support to her.

When Tharoor chooses to portray Indira Gandhi as Duryodhani, it follows that her two close aides R.K. Dhawan and Siddharth Shankar Ray are given the identity of Dushasana and Shakuni. The parallelism holds good as Shakuni and Dushasana of the epic were mainly responsible for tempting Duryodhan to get intoxicated with power.

Krishna is one character from the epic for whom there is no parallel drawn from history. His identity is kept vague and ambiguous. He is referred to as "the local MLA and the Kaurava Party Secretary for the taluk. His name is D. Krishna Parthasarathy" (327). "Arjuna found himself entranced. In Krishna he found qualities he had never seen in any man nor sought in any woman. He was irresistibly drawn to Krishna's almost magical combination of self-possession and extroversion, mischief and maturity, joy and judgment and his rare gift of the common touch" (328).

According to Tharoor, Krishna was too satisfied with his life in Gokarnam as a hero and MLA to seek a place in the national Parliament. He fuses myth and history while referring to his parent as freedom fighters who were in jail when he was born. Tharoor, like several other earlier critics, refrains from investing Krishna with divinity. He fictionalized Krishna's miraculous powers into incredible intelligence. To Tharoor, Krishna represents the intellectuals and eminent statesmen. He calls him "Krishna the thinker" (356) and remarks, "India has too many Krishnas. His brilliance burned himself out without illuminating the country. He cannot reach the top" (414).

Such a remark throws into reconsideration the role of Krishna in the epic. Krishna with his amazing brilliance, shrewdness and diplomacy could have possibly brought about the unity of the Pandavas and the Kauravas and averted the tragedy of war. Perhaps he wanted to establish that evil cannot flourish for a long time and that the destruction of evil necessitates the loss of some good also. Prema Nandakumar remarks that the depiction of Krishna is a challenge to Tharoor: "Flying straight into the face of the *Mahabharata* tale, Tharoor gets the full blast of the legendary characters and is hard put to assign them all proper riches in twentieth century India. Krishna definitely eludes him. There is but a brief appearance of D. Krishna Parthasarathy Menon as a local party Secretary whose grant of termless sari to Draupadi proves to be a phenomenon too much for Tharoor's ready to-spin-anything brain" (21).

Descriptive details point to Madhava Menon, other details suggest that he is a power to reckon with, more than a personality called Madhava Menon. His involvement with *Matru Bhoomi*, *Malayala Manorama* and such other journals that protested against Emergency could be symbolic of Krishna's intimacy with Arjun who in turn stands for the Press. The Krishna of the epic looms large in the mind of the reader and hence no parallel.

In fictionalizing the epic Tharoor not only reinterprets the major characters of the epic but also recasts certain events. In his "Afterword" to the novel he admits to having taken "far too many liberties with the epic" (149). He adds that the responsibility for this entirely fictional version is of course his alone. The fictional strategy compels him to include certain events from the epic that have no parallel in history. Due to compulsions of history, Tharoor has to introduce certain events that did not find a place in the epic. In both instances Tharoor has to resort to direct narration. For example, the early part of the epic comprising Parashar-Satyavati union, birth of Vyasa, Shantanu's relationship with Ganga, birth of the Prince Ganga Datta, Shantanu's love for Satyavati and their marriage, Bhishma's vow of celibacy, birth of the sons of Satyavati, Bhishma's trigamous mission to Kashi to produce the brides for Satyavati's sons are all narrated directly. All these events have no parallels in history and so they are narrated in the mode of story telling.

As far as the political history of modern India is concerned Tharoor's novel spans a period of more than half a century from the time of Gandhi's involvement in freedom struggle upto the fall of Janata Government and the return of Indira Gandhi to power. Gandhiji's involvement in three significant struggles during the course of 1917 and early 1918 in Champaran in Bihar, Ahmedabad and in Kheda in Gujarat is directly reported.

Referring to these events, the historian Bipan Chandra says that "these struggles served as a demonstration of Gandhiji's style and method of politics to the country at large" (181). Gandhiji's Satyagraha as a powerful strategy to achieve the goal in the early years of the struggle for freedom is appreciated by the novelist. He found it to be a "beacon of hope and strength of our subjugation" (105). What follows is an ironic understatement, a sort of parody typical of a postmodern metafiction.: "fasts have never worked half as well anywhere else as they have in India. Only Indians could have devised a method of political bargaining based on the threat to harm to yourself rather than to your opponent" (105). The tone again shifts to a serious one recording the contrast between the past and the present: everything has changed today: "All we are left with is the drama without the sacrifice and isn't that a metaphor for Indian politics today?" (105)

Some of the events of history are either parodied or presented in the mock-heroic style. The Great Dandi March is parodied as the Great Mango March. The element of parody makes the reader look back at the past and revise his opinion. In the novel, some of the leaders of the Kaurava party did not agree with Gangaji in making "salt" an issue. "Pandu was aghast . . . making mango an issue when there are other vital issues" (118). But it is acknowledged that only "Gangaji could dramatize and ennoble the most insignificant causes when he chose to" (121). Later Pandu admitted that the Mango March did fire the people's imagination (121). Other important events of history fictionalized by Tharoor are Jalianwala Bagh Massacre, Civil Disobedience, Quit India Movement, Partition, Indo-China War, Liberation of Goa, Bangladesh War, Emergency and so on.

One of the events that have been recast by Tharoor is the death of Gandhi. Tharoor refers to Amba as the assassin of Gangaji implying a parallel between Amba-Shikhandin and Godse. Amba's rebirth as Shikhandin is presented in the modern idiom. Tharoor makes Amba undergo sex change through a simple medical treatment and thus the original myth of Amba's begging a boon from Shiva to kill Bhishma is altered to suit the modern context.

Tharoor does not blame Nathuram Godse solely for the death of Gandhi. He makes a critical reassessment of Gandhi's life and points out that his own sense of failure brought about his death rather than the bullets of Godse. Shikhandin of the novel points out to Gangaji that his life is a waste: "'Look at the mess you've made.' A hand swept out to the world beyond, 'you don't still want to live, do you?'" (232). While dying Gangaji groaned out of the words, "I . . . have . . . failed" (234).

The novelist's presentation of Gandhi's death offers significant insights into Gandhi's own inner agony at the partition of the country and his failure to avert the disaster. The implied analogy startles the reader into a reappraisal of Bhishma's life in the epic. It becomes obvious that Bhishma's life was also a fruitless sacrifice as all his efforts to prop up the Kuru dynasty were in vain. He also failed to avert the catastrophe of the war. Irawati Karve asks if Bhishma had accomplished anything by keeping up the vows (29). A boy named Arjun brought some water to the dying Gangaji and this reference is in keeping with the original epic.

As in the epic, Karna does receive the blessings of Gangaji at the time of his death, "and as the unacknowledged son of Kunti rose to leave, the story goes, a hand slipped out from the shroud and graced the shoulder. Gangaji disagreed with no man more profoundly, yet he would not deny Mohammed Ali Karna his blessing when he asked for it" (235).

The reader is compelled to interrogate the epic whether Bhishma's treatment of Karna was fair and whether he should not have given his blessings to Karna to lead the Kaurava army. In the epic, Bhishma never gave Karna any due recognition for his heroism and valour or for his skill in archery.

Yet another instance of fictional recasting of events is Tharoor's treatment of Drona's revenge of Drupad. In the novel Drona of modern India is Jaya Prakash Narayan. The use of a part of the name itself is an explicit indication of the parallel. Tharoor presents two different versions of Jayaprakash Drona's treatment of Heaslop. According to Linda Hutcheon, it is part of his narrative strategy to offer two alternate versions in a postmodern fiction (85).

In the first version, the narrative presents the imaginary episode of JP Drona settling his old scores with Heaslop. When Heaslop comes to him with an appeal for one-time special grant in partial restitution for losses suffered to private property in performance of service related, JP Drona the then Minister of State of Administrative Reforms not only rejected the appeal but paid him some coins towards contribution to the collection for unfortunate Heaslop. The narrator concludes: "No, in fact it didn't happen that way. Sometimes I wish it had, that Indian had proved capable for paying the Raj back if you'll pardon the metaphor, in its own coin, . . . Revenge was one quality absent in the way he and other members of independent Indian government treated their former masters" (242). The wish to pay British in their own coin is also a protest against the colonizers.

Such instances give a postcolonial aspect to the novel. The passage quoted above is an expression of the desire to write back to the colonial masters. Referring to the episode Viney Kirpal observes, that Indians should have decolonized their minds:

> Had Indian leaders and intellectuals shown more "violence" towards their ex-masters they would have liberated themselves from the colonizers' domination. In the absence of spiritual, true decolonization, Indians (particularly the intellectuals) had remained passive and stereotypical in their thinking, always taking their cue from the west. (52)

Tharoor sometimes gives a symbolic interpretation to the events of the epic. The Svayamwar of Draupadi is an event that acquires symbolic significance in the context of history. According to the narrator, the beauty of the epic heroine is no myth but a fact: "Draupadi Mokrasi met the Pandavas for the first time and dazzled them and all the other young men in the camp with her radiance" (311). The Svayamwar of Draupadi is compared to the system of parliamentary democracy, upheld by periodical elections as against the Presidential form of Government. Critics of the *Mahabharata* such as V.S. Sukthankar have given a symbolic interpretation of the original event of Draupadi's marriage of the Pandavas in the epic itself.

> Thus, for example, there is . . . in the crucial instance no historical basis for the polyandrous marriage of Draupadi with the Pandava brothers, which is to be understood only symbolically. The Pandavas themselves symbolize the undivided or joint family; and Draupadi, their common wife in the story stands for the ideal embodiment and representation of the unconditional unity of the family. (21)

In the epic there is a mythical interpretation of Draupadi's polyandrous marriage. According to an ancient myth Draupadi prayed to

Shiva and asked for a husband five times and Shiva granted her wish. Consequently Draupadi was blessed with five husbands. Tharoor fictionalizes the ancient myth by drawing an analogy between the polyandry of Draupadi and the multicultural multi-religious feature of Indian democracy:

> 'I pray to Shiva,' Draupadi said, 'to Jehovah, to the Virgin mother of adoptive parents, to the Allah of the Muslims and—she blushed, in acknowledgement of her maternal faith—to the Archbishop of Canterbury.'
>
> 'Poor confused child' I said. They have all answered your prayers.
>
> Once it was clear that Draupadi had brought her five husbands upon herself by her five prayers, all resistance to the multiple marriages melted. (316)

The fictional rendering of Draupadi's Svayamwar slightly deviates from the epic in making Duryodhani suggest the idea of Svayamwar to Draupadi. Though a minor deviation, it amounts to distorting, as in the original epic, Duryodhana is one of the suitors of Draupadi during the Svayamwar. But such distortions are inevitable if the novelist has to honour the context of history.

Two of the issues related to or consequent to the polyandrous marriage of Draupadi to Pandavas are also dealt with by the novelist. The first of these is the treatment meted out to Bhim's wife and sister of Hidimba. Tharoor makes an ironic commentary on the predicament of Hidimba's sister. He observes that Kunti's treatment of Hidimba's sister is one discordant note he had so far omitted to strike:

> This was true; the Pandavas under their mother were terribly self-sufficient with the self-obsession that sometimes accompanies self-possession. It had not been easy for her to belong. Perhaps the only way to belong in that family was Draupadi's. It was ironic but true. One Swayamwara drove out another. And so Ganapathi, Bhim's wife left our story, never to return. And have you noticed? We still don't know her name. (316)

The narrator's comment on the plight of Hidimba's sister raises questions about Kunti's treatment of Bhim's wife. In the epic,

Hidimba is described as belonging to the Rakshasa tribe. Then, it is to be examined if Kunti was nourishing racial prejudice against Hidimba's sister. Tharoor suggests that she sank into anonymity after the Svayamwar of Draupadi.

The second of these issues relates to the arrangement of the Pandavas to share Draupadi equally among themselves, as it came as an injunction from their mother Kunti. In the political context they stand for the five supportive systems of democracy namely, Law and Justice, Army, Press, IAS & IFS. The marriage is symbolic of the protection given to Draupadi Mokrasi by the Pandavas who guaranteed their unity by the rigid rule that punished any intrusion with a year's banishment.

The narrator refers to Arjun's violation of the rule under extraordinary circumstances and the consequent exile he had to suffer only to question the justness of Arjun's brothers sharing her when he alone had the right to take her as his wife. "Arjun could not help wondering as he took his leave of a tearful Draupadi whether Yudhishtir would have been able to win Draupadi's hand by himself. And think of Draupadi abandoned by the man she had loved and wanted to marry . . . a curiously unjust world" (321-22).

Arjun's exile and travels are all symbolic of the Indian press presenting a wide coverage of the landscape, the people and their problems. The novelist's insight into the rise of violence in the country is worth consideration:

> He saw the range and immensity of India and all its concerns. In rural Bengal he learned of the rage and frustration that led middleclass young intellectuals to throw bombs at lower-class old policemen. . . . And then Arjun saw the tortured Naxalites languish in their cockroach-infested prison cells and did not blame them whey they recanted. (322)

The episode of Bhima's encounter with Hidimba is yet another instance of fictional recasting of events. Bhima-Hidimba encounter is a symbolic representation of India's conquest of Goa, a Portuguese colony. The then Defence Minister V.K. Krishna Menon "persuaded his Premier that it was time to embark on a new course. The armed forces of the Indian Republic would take over the defiant but ill-defended colony (296).

Tharoor alternates between the modes of prose and verse while narrating the episode of Bhima-Hidimba. The story of taking over of Comeas (fictionalized name of Goa) is narrated in prose and the tale from the epic is presented in verse form. The alternating modes are well appropriated for alternating between history and the epic. While Bhima was fighting Hidimba, his sister was making passionate entreaties to Kunti to wed her son. The tale of romance between Hidimba's sister and Bhima has all the elements of a comic play that Tharoor chooses a mock-epic tone, much to the amusement of the reader. Bhima is shocked when his mother asks him to marry the giant's sister: "I can't believe it. As I fought, you were arranging my marriage?" (299).

Tharoor draws a parallel between the episode of disrobing Draupadi and violating the norms of democracy during the regime of Indira Gandhi. The chronological sequence of the game of dice preceding the episode of disrobing has been altered by Tharoor to suit the context (as lifting of Emergency is followed by calling for elections). The reference is to the public humiliation and disgrace suffered by Draupadi when Dushasana assaulted her modesty in the Kuru Sabha. Tharoor recasts this event into the context of history when the norms of democracy were unscrupulously violated by the then Primer Minister Indira Gandhi. The imposition of Emergency and harassment of her political adversaries has been referred to by the historians as the dark period of Indian democracy, when political culture sank to the lowest depths. The comparison between history and the epic converges on the point of unethical practices adopted by Duryodhana of the epic and his female counterpart in modern India. The metaphor of bleeding serves to highlight the excesses of emergency:

> Can I acknowledge the little hurts and bruises and burns I had spotted on her arms and hand and face at each visit to her home and dismiss them, as Kunti did, as minor kitchen mishaps. Can I admit the terrible suspicion that her own husbands were ill-treating her, exploiting her, even ignoring her and still excuse myself for having done nothing about it? (374)

The parallelism, at once brings out the novelist's deploring the failure of Pandavas, in no uncertain terms, to protect the honour of Draupadi of the epic and the failure of political leaders to uphold the ideals of democracy in modern India. Thus fictionalizing history is an effective strategy to expose the causes of decadence in Hastinapur-Delhi of ancient and modern India. Tharoor holds up Siddharth Shankar Ray, the Shakuni of history and R.K. Dhawan, the Dushasana of history, the two close aides of the then Prime Minister Indira Gandhi responsible for the acts of atrocity.

Commenting on Tharoor's re-rendering of the episode of disrobing, Prema Nandakumar says, the Tamil poet Bharathi's *Panchali Sapatham* also portrays Draupadi as a symbol of Indian womanhood:

> This injustice done to Draupadi is actually the collective wrong to which the Indian woman had been subjected since several centuries. . . . His Draupadi also became an image of ageless India. [. . .] Several decades after Bharathi's brilliant symbolization, Shashi Tharoor has taken up the same symbol and handled with sufficient care to produce *The Great Indian Novel*. Bharathi's dream was an Independent India. Tharoor sees the reality of Independent India also as the desecrated Draupadi in the Kuru court. (19)

The narrator seems to implicate Kunti for her indifference to the assault of Draupadi's modesty, dismissing the cuts and bruises as kitchen mishaps. The reader is made to reassess the relationship between Kunti and Draupadi in the epic.

The game of dice is used by Tharoor as a metaphor for elections and the element of chance is the point of analogy. In the epic the game of dice is a bait to trap the Pandavas and the suggestion comes from Shakuni. Yudhishthir accepts the invitation to play dice but emerges not as a winner but as a great loser. He loses not only the kingdom but his wife and brothers too. In the novel, Tharoor deviates from the epic and shows Duryodhani as the loser due to compulsions of history. On the contrary, the Yudhishthir of modern India Morarji Desai emerges victorious in the 1977 elections and becomes the Prime Minister. But the victory of Desai was only a short- lived glory. By drawing a parallel between Yudhishtir and Desai, Tharoor brings out the weaknesses of both,

Yudhishtir was self-obsessed and he failed to discern the impression he made on others. Morarji Desai's eccentricities like advocating auto-urine therapy made him the laughing stock of the nation and his Front was crumbling. "The Indian people gave themselves the privilege of replacing a determined collected tyrant with an indeterminate collection of tyros" (402). Ultimately the dice of government was flung back at the Kauravas' feet.

The lac-house episode is an event that finds no parallel in history and so the novelist resorts to direct narration. But the narrator's comments on the use of STOP in telegrams give rise to much humour. Vidura's warning to the Pandavas through an allegorical tale is parodied in the telegram sent by Vidur of history.

> FOR YUDHISHTIR CARE GPO VARANAVATA STOP YOUR LATEST ASTROLOGICAL FORECAST STOP BE WARY TROJAN HOUSE STOP GUARD AGAINST HEADLESS PARSON STOP DON'T LET ON COLON NO IMMEDIATE REARRANGED GARDEN STOP AM SENDING RABBIT TO HELP BURROW STOP TRAVEL BROADENS THE HORIZONS STOP LET STARS LIGHT YOUR PATH STOP UNCLE VIDUR. (283)

The suggestion to dig up a cave and escape from the danger in the lac house built of inflammable materials is provided by the arrangement to send the rabbit to help burrow. The lac house episode could be a parallel to Indira Gandhi's ways of getting rid of her adversaries.

Such instances of using the episodes from the epic to highlight the personality traits are quite often resorted to by the novelist. Duryodhana's unsuccessful attempts at eliminating the Pandavas, by poisoning Bhim's food and of pushing him into the river are all parodied to expose Indira Gandhi's ways of eliminating her political adversaries: 'Even at the age of twelve overkill was already her problem' (55).

The 1969 Presidential Election is another event in history that has no parallel in the epic. Tharoor mythicises history to focus on the unethical behaviour of Indira Gandhi. He fictionalizes history while referring to the event. The Kaurava Party had announced an official candidate for the post of President. But the incumbent PM proposed Ekalavya's name as against the official nominee and sought a conscience vote. The results were in favour of Ekalavya. And the Kaurava Party split into Kaurava (R) and Kaurava (O). The obvious parallels in history are Neelam Sanjeeva Reddy who was the official nominee of the Congress Party and V.V. Giri who was chosen by Indira Gandhi to oppose him. The breach of party discipline by Indira Gandhi led to the split of the party as Congress (O) and Congress (I). Tharoor suggests that the unscrupulous acts of Indira Gandhi weakened Indian democracy. The use of metaphor is effective in bringing out the deteriorating situation. "And Draupadi Mokrasi was diagnosed as asthmatic, her breath coming sometimes in short gasps, the dead air trapped in her bronchia struggling to expel itself, her chest heaving with the effort to breathe freely" (352).

Satire and humour are blended and fused into the narrative wherever the novelist resorts to parody. For instance, Kanika's advice to Dhritarashtra in the epic is parodied in the verse form:

> Stealth and discretion are the means
> To employ in making plans;
> A clever king, though, never, leans
> In trust on another man.
> Pretend! Conceal! Find out! Mistrust!
> These are the vital things;
> Maintain a cheerful outer crust
> But permit no rival kings. (271)

In the novel the advice given by the scheming minister was overheard by Priya Duryodhani. "She was glad her idealistic father had some less idealistic friends. Dhritarashtra might forget Kanika's advice but Priya Duryodhani would remember every word of the acerbic High Commissioner's brutal counsel. And she would not hesitate to act on it" (273).

Tharoor uses the same context to highlight the scheming mind of V.K. Krishna Menon and the ruthless determination of Indira Gandhi since her early life. Tharoor's portrayal of V.K. Krishna Menon as a Machiavellian villain is a reflection of contemporary opinion, a changed perspective of the past: Kanika admits to taking his lessons from the wise men of the past. "In questions of political judgment, Prime Minister, I am something of a traditionalist, he said at last. I go back to the lessons of the Arthashastra from which Machiavelli plagiarized so effectively and the Shantiparvan of Vyasa" (270). The choice of Kanikà from the epic to represent Krishna Menon seems to be well-appropriated to create the fictional parallel.

An event in the *Mahabharata* that does not find a parallel in the novel is the death of Karna. While depicting Karna's death, the novelist just makes an indirect reference to the fateful circumstances in which he had to face the arrows of Arjun—when he was mending the wheels of his chariot. "But anyway, the actual climax was rather pathetic. Seems his official vehicle got stuck in the mud somewhere on an inspection tour, Karna barked at the driver, which only made the poor fool more nervous, so nervous he revived the engine too strongly and got the wheel embedded even more deeply in the mud" (277).

Tharoor doesn't seem to question the ethicality of Arjun's act of killing Karna in the epic when Karna was at a disadvantage. Several critics of the *Mahabharata* have deplored the act of Arjuna killing Karna in an ignoble manner. V.S. Sukthankar while summing up the views of Western critics says: "observe how these righteous Pandavas, the supposed souls of Dharma, are able to win the war only by Adharma, by a series of frauds of at least by some very shabby and unchivalrous acts, which no right-thinking person would hesitate to condemn" (12). Karna's fictional counterpart Jinnah died in Pakistan after partition. He was also driven by a sense of failure as he could not protect the integrity of his theistic state which was again hacked off into two. It is a historical necessity that the circumstances of the two were different at the time of their death and that leaves the novelist with no choice of a parallel.

Yet another event in the epic that finds no parallel in history is the death of Ashwathama. Through the use of parody, Tharoor highlights the ignoble act of Yudhishthir uttering a lie that Ashwathama is dead by falsely referring to the elephant named Ashwathama:

> "You, Yudhishtir, you of all people. I believed you could never lie."
> "You believed right, V. Viji." Yudhishtir said implacably, I didn't lie this time either—when I said Ashwathama was dead, I was

> speaking the truth. Before leaving the house I caught a cockroach in the closet, named it Ashwathama and crushed it under my prime ministerial dispatch box. So Viji I did not lie to Drona. I never said it was his son who had died. (410)

This is an instance of parodying the myth to satirize the meanness and triviality of the act of Yudhishtir to hit Drona on his vulnerable spot.

In the process of fictionalizing the epic, Tharoor, at times, has to distort the original version to serve the intent of his art. The Drona-Ekalavya episode is an instance of conscious deviation from the original. The novelist says in "The Relevance of the *Mahabharata* in Today's India," that such deviations were inevitable:

> My various literary and less than literary devices serve an attempt to look at political history through the refraction of two different kinds of light. One is, of course, the light cast by the past, by the values taught to us in our mythology, by the examples set by the *Mahabharata*. The other is the light cast by a satirical view of the present, which by deliberate simplification and fictionalization (one might even say conscious distortion) throws certain trends and issues into sharper relief than history makes possible. This certainly applies to the real life "parallels" with the *Mahabharata* that reviewers have been quick to seize upon, but it is also valid where no parallel exists. (Lal 1:347)

In the epic Ekalavya cuts off his thumb to pay the fees demanded by his master. But in Tharoor's novel, Ekalavya refuses to give the fee to his Guru:

> Drona advances upon him, bringing his face so close to the boy's that the hairs of his beard graze Ekalavya's nose. If you do not pay your guru the fee he seeks, you are unworthy of what he has taught you,' he snarls, his spittle flecking the boy's forehead. Ekalavya stands his ground, but swallows his dark face burning darker in his dismay. 'I'm sorry sir, but I cannot destroy my life and my mother's to pay your fee,' he says faintly but firmly. (199)

Tharoor seems to alter the Ekalavya story to satirize the unjust demands of the guru which need not be fulfilled at the cost of ruining one's life. The Ekalavya of the epic would not have protested against the discriminations based on caste / class consideration;

perhaps the twentieth century attitude has changed. Due to the upliftment and empowerment of the socially-downtrodden, there is a tendency to refuse to accept the superiority based on caste/ community. One could probably find subaltern echoes in Tharoor's Ekalavya. Tharoor admits that the "Ekalavya story had to be changed to make a twentieth century point" (Lal 1:347).

Vanashree Tripathi's observation of Karna's protest parallels Tharoor's observation of Ekalavya. She says, "The *Mahabharata* has already recognized that the heredity-determined hegemony is unfair. Karna's assertion, that a human being's worth must be judged by his actions, virtues and merits and not by birth, is emblematic of the righteous protest of the oppressed groups in the society" (123). But Manoj Das in "The Spell of the *Mahabharata*" says that the episode of Ekalavya is often projected as an instance of the discriminatory conduct of the privileged towards the ordinary Ekalavya:

> But the question involved in Ekalavya's case is not varna as much as the welfare of Ekalavya himself. In his enthusiasm he has got hold of the physical and occult science of archery all right but he knows nothing about the code of conduct that must temper this knowledge. . . . Ekalavya had applied his archery on a dog which had the audacity of barking at him. He shut the creature's mouth with arrows. Reduced to dumbness the dog ran to Drona and drew his attention to its plight. We have to remember the role of the Guru of yore. His first concern was the soul of the disciple; a lesson had no value if it brought about a degradation in the disciple's consciousness if it merely gave a boost to his ego (I).

This according to Manoj Das is an instance of significant silences in the epic making certain situations vulnerable to moral challenges. Manoj Das's interpretation gives the reader fresh insights into the episode.

Bhim-Baka episode is another example of deviation verging on distortion in Tharoor's novel. In the novel Baka is depicted as a wrestling champion who had pitched his tent in the city of Ekachakra. This is a symbolic representation of the Chinese aggression triggering Indo-China war in 1962. Baka represents China and the city of Ekachakra (single chakra symbolic of Indian flag) stands for India. In the epic Bhim conquers Baka and crushes him to death. But in the novel neither Bhim confronts Baka nor is Baka conquered. Instead of Bhim, it is Sahadev who is sent to tackle Baka. Sahadev in the novel stands for Indian Foreign Services. Tharoor alters the characters and the event to fulfil the requirements of his satire and to honour the facts of history. Baka, in Tharoor's novel, subdues Sahadev. Bhim's infatuation with Ghatotkacha at that time can be equated with the ill-equipped army. In the fictional rendering of the event, description of the wrestling match shows the humiliating defeat of Sahadev:

> A cheer went up from the assembled crowds as Sahadev stepped diffidently into the ring, his slim, lithe and lightly muscled figure, a startling contrast to the gleaming oiled barrel of solid flesh that was Bakasura. Sahadev turned to acknowledge the cheers and heard them become a roar, a roar, though he was to realize it only too late, of fear and warning [. . .] and suddenly found himself being picked up from behind, spun above Bakasura's head like the blades of a human helicopter and flung bodily into the row of seats occupied by the judges of the contest. As he passed out amidst their screams and the splintering of chairs, the last word he heard was Bakasura's chest-thumping snarl: Next ! (303)

India's deplorable debacle in the Indo-China war has been rerendered by the fusion of fact and fiction as well as myth and history. Tharoor seems to echo the opinion of the majority that Indian foreign policy was so flawed that it ultimately brought about the disgraceful defeat of the Indians. Kunti was puzzled. She asked her sons how they could allow it to happen. "How could you allow it to happen?," says Tharoor, "was a question many of us in the Kaurava Party could not resist asking Dhritarashtra when the Chakars invaded, tossed our ill-fed, ill-clad, ill-shod jawans contemptuously aside and inexorably erased the Big Mac Line" (304).

According to Tharoor, the Chinese even exposed the shallowness of our international pretensions to the world: "They even shook the credibility of Dhritarashtra's non-alignment, for our blind Prime Minister panicked enough to welcome the offer of a squadron of fighter planes and pilot from the superpower whose alliances he had earlier consistently spurned" (304).

The military unpreparedness and the flawed foreign policies are cited as the cause for India's defeat in the war. Tharoor also records the popular opinion of Nehru's death brought about by the disaster: "The military humiliation not only shattered his self-esteem; it broke his heart. His decline was gradual but decisive. . . He did not last long after that" (305).

In the process of re-rendering the events of the past, Tharoor resorts to dream-narration as part of the narrative strategy. He fuses myth and history in a dream sequence while drawing a parallel between the slaying of Jarasandh and the hacking off of Karnistan. M.K. Chaudhuri commenting on the strategy says:

> In his fictional rendering of the history of India of post-Gandhi period, Tharoor makes a more skilful use of the mythic setting by relating the past and the present in a dream. By replacing the past vertically on the horizontal present, he integrates a number of key episodes of the *Mahabharata* into the story, a couple of which are slightly modified, in order to project important political events of the post Independence period [. . .] the tearing off of the body of Jarasandha into two by Bhima reflects the dismembering of Pakistan and the creation of Bangladesh. (111)

The great Hacker-off had to witness the hacking off of his land into two, the metaphor of 'hacking-off' is drawn from Karna's hacking off of the shield to Indra in the epic. It is well-appropriated to comment on the partition of India and later the division of Pakistan:

> I dreamt, for instance, of Karnistan's Jarasandha coming into being like the sons of our mythical king Brihadratha—the fruit, quite literally, of his twin wives. Brihadrath's wives had conceived after years of childlessness by each eating half a mango given as a boon to their husband by the sage Kaushik, and each had produced half a boy. The two halves had fused into the strong and independent Jarasandha, whose great physical prowess was limited by one fatal flaw the fact that his body, being a fusion of two separate parts could one day be broken into two again. And in my dream Duryodhani was a queen who resolved to conduct the Rajasuya sacrifice and crown himself Empress. (356)

There is a slight deviation from the original here. In the epic it is Yudhishtir who conducted the Rajasuya Yajna and crowned himself as the Great Emperor. The glory of invincibility that came to Yudhishtir was the cause of Duryodhana's humiliation, provoking jealousy. But Tharoor distorts the episode and makes Duryodhani conduct the Rajasuya to crown herself the Empress. The distortion was necessitated by the context of history.

The Bangladesh war and India's support to Bangladesh ultimately led to deifying of Indira Gandhi as an Empress and a Mother Goddess:

> India accorded Duryodhani its ultimate accolade. She was not just deified, she was maternalised. This woman who had never married and who looked incapable of producing or sustaining human life, became known as Ma Duryodhani and Duryodhani Amma to a people who saw in her the embodiment of the female principle of Shakti the power and the strength of a national Mother Goddess. (355)

In the novel the great victory was made possible only due to the endeavours of Bhim the soldier, Arjun the spy, and Krishna the thinker (356). Tharoor seems to suggest that a strong army with a network of intelligence systems planned by intellectuals could have contributed to the triumph. The contribution of Bhim, Arjun and Krishna is true of the epic too. Tharoor seems to echo the opinion of Irawati Karve that Yudhishthir had no military prowess himself and all his achievements were possible only because of Bhim's valour, Arjun's heroism and Krishna's intelligence.

The narrator's final comment, "Thus, Ganapathi, was Jarasandha slain in my dream and thus when I opened my eyes was Karnistan, the Hacked-Off Land, itself hacked in two." (356) The passage seems to implicitly suggest the working of nemesis as in a Greek play. But it is far from the intention of Tharoor to moralise any tale.

Certain evens of history find no parallel in the epic; for instance, the accession of Kashmir is directly narrated. All other vents of history encompassing the decline and fall of Indira Gandhi, such as the decision to impose Emergency, the ill-treatment and imprisonment of her political opponents, Jaya Prakash Narain's open revolt against her repressive measures are all presented in chronological sequence. The siege in the novel stands for the emergency imposed by Indira Gandhi following her impeachment in the Allahabad judgement. The narrative covers the period upto the fall of Janata Government and Indira Gandhi's return to power and finally her assassination in 1984.

It is significant to note that Tharoor does not conclude his tale as VV tells Ganapathi that stories never end. "The story of the *Mahabharata* does not end on the field of the battle. What happens afterwards is tragedy, suffering, futility, death, which underlines the only moral of that battle and the epic that there are no real victors. Everyone loses at the end" (391). Perpetual struggle marks not only the epic and history but life in general: "This election is not Kurukshetra; life is Kurukshetra. History is Kurukshetra. The struggle between dharma and adharma is a struggle, our nation and each of us in it engages in on every single day of our existence" (391).

Commenting on Tharoor's fusion of history and myth and drawing parallels between the two, E.V. Ramakrishnan in "The Politics of Language and the Language of Politics: Anita Desai's *In Custody*, Shashi Tharoor's *The Great Indian Novel* and O.V. Vijayan's *The Saga of Dharmapuri*" says: 'By equating Nathuram Godse with Shikhandin or Jaya Prakash Narayan with Drona, no particular insight into the nature of Indian society is provided. In recasting the 2000 year-old tale in twentieth century terms, Tharoor's parallels remain far-fetched and synthetic with no intrinsic power to illuminate" (62).

But Ayyappa Panikar observes that "whatever intertextuality is preserved between the epic and the novel is sustained by the creative irreverence of the re-teller seeking justification and support from the archetypal narrator of the epic himself" (16).

In a typical postmodernist device of self-reflexivity, very often the narrator VV, by exchanging his views with his scribe Ganapathi, comments on the art of narration itself. Commenting on the use of dream-narration as a device of subversion, VV tells Ganapathi, "sometimes, Ganapathi, dreams enable you to see reality more clearly" (383). The last march of Yudhishtir and the other Pandavas to heaven is also a dream of the narrator.

The relevance of the epic framework has been commended by M.K. Chaudhury:

> The *Mahabharata* is a unitary national myth that perceives itself as totality and provides for Tharoor's novel that most appropriate allegorical background to project modern Indian situation. Tharoor uses the mythic setting of the ancient epic to foreground the eternal present, the continuance of the historical process from India's remote past to the present. (105)

Both history and the epic are interpreted differently, adapted to the shifts in the socio-political milieu. Tharoor's reworking of the past may not be acceptable to some. P.K. Rajan in "History and Myth in *The Great Indian Novel*" says:

> History is in fact an ensemble of the lived experiences of a people, and a sense of this experience is precisely what is missing in the fictional world of *The Great Indian Novel*. . . . The novel does not, therefore provide an interpretation of reality in terms of myth, it only parodies myth in terms of contemporary facts—a method which is at times felt to be forced, arbitrarily contrived and artificial with the result that the parallelisms tend to be unconvincing or seem to crumble at certain critical points. (28)

The narrator himself has stated that he did not aim at total parallelism and admits of the difficulty of interpreting the past. VV wonders, "how much one may select, interpret and arrange to living past before truth is jeopardized by inaccuracy" (164). Tharoor concentrates on select figures and events in the past. T.N. Dhar says, V.V.'s final, clinching statement ties up his observations on the problematics of historical reconstructions:

> for every tale I have told you, every perception I have conveyed, there are a hundred equally valid alternatives I have omitted and of which you are unaware. I make no apologies for this. This is my story of the India I know, with its biases, sections, omissions, distortions all mine. . . . Every Indian must for ever carry with him, in his head and heart his own history of India. (373)

What Tharoor does is, as earlier stated, to interrogate history and the epic, provoking the reader to re-examine his perception of the cultural past. Sethuraman in "Literature after Theory: A Case Study," says, "*The Great Indian Novel* has helped us the readers to raise the relevant questions regarding ideology/ class/ race/ gender/ social reality" (131).

The choice of subtitles reinforces the idea that Tharoor possesses what Eliot calls "historical consciousness." Viney Kirpal in "Politics and Philosophy in *The Great Indian Novel*" observes. "In *The Great Indian Novel*, the titles of most chapters are a play, a parody on the titles of famous novels and traditional Indian literature, suggesting thereby the presence of the entire tradition of literature—modern and ancient in the writing of this novel" (20).

Therefore, the sub-titles can be regarded as a sort of intertext. According to Lynda Hutcheon, the use of footnotes, written documents, chapter headings and epigraphs as a paratext is a distinct feature of historiographic metafiction. These devices, according to Hutcheon, move at once in two directions: "to remind us of the narrativity (and fictionality) of the primary text and to assert its factuality and historicity" (85). The titles of the eighteen books are parodic inversions of several well-known literary works. Forbidden Fruit, The Son also Rises, Midnight's Parents/Him—or The Far Power Villain (*The Far Pavillions* by MM Kaye), Darkness at Dawn (*Darkness at Noon* by Arthur Koestler). The man who could not be king, Passages through India, The Bungle Book or The Reign of Error are some of the titles that are parodied. The Rigged Veda is one of the titles which according to Balaswamy, subverts the Rig Veda, suggesting the changeless nature of corruption in independent India. He says that the novel is a "brilliant exercise in the reassessment of contemporary history without resorting to any platitudes or certitudes" (236).

The narrator uses the dream sequence once again towards the end of the novel and makes Yudhishthir express his surprise to find Duryodhani in Heaven:

> Yama (Dharma) corrects him saying, 'it was all an illusion, my son. You will no more be condemned to an eternity of misery than Duryodhani will enjoy perpetual contentment.' . . . 'No more certi-

> tudes' he called out, desperately to the receding figure. 'Accept doubt and diversity. . . . Derive your standards from the world around you and not from a heritage whose relevance must be constantly tested. Reject equally the sterility of ideologies and the passionate perceptions of those, who think themselves infallible.' (147)

Tharoor does refrain from endorsing certainties and drawing conclusions. Such uncertainties and avoiding the notion of closure is a perceptible postmodern trend. He recognizes and endorses the multiplicity of truth. Yudhishthir in the novel declares that there is more than one truth. Tharoor has a pluralistic concept of truth and a contextual perception of history. M.F. Salat observes that history is made by winners:

> The losers either have no history or have one that is given to them by the winners. Hence, the 1857 uprising in India against the British colonial rule comes to be labelled as a mutiny rather than as a revolution which is what it actually was and the richer and much older American culture gets branded as savage and barbaric in British colonial historiography. As the historian Hayden White quite rightly claims that historiography is a poetic construct and as such is neither scientific nor objective. (126)

Since history is written from the victor's point of view, it cannot be an objective record. The narrator VV (Tharoor) is both a witness to history and a participant in it. The novel is an attempt to revisit the past only to contest it. VV says: "But that is another story, eh, Ganapathi? And one we shall come to in due course. Never fear, you can dip your twitching nose into that slice of our history too. 'But let us tidy up some genealogy first' (25). Tharoor is well aware of the difficulties in the task. He says, "The yoking of the *Mahabharata* to modern history restricted some of my fictional options; as the novel progressed. I was obliged to abandon novelistic conventions and develop characters who were merely walking metaphors" (Lal 1:347).

M.K. Chaudhury says that, "the purpose of parallelism [. . .] like the general purpose of imagery is to transfer the usual perception of an object into the sphere of new perception—that it is to make a unique semantic modification" (113).

So, what Tharoor does is to modify our perception of both history and the epic. He does not assert that his view of the past has been objective. The last lines of the novel are very significant, conveying the message that the past is constantly reviewed and reassessed and that the fact of today will become the myth of tomorrow. Even his account of the past is subject to interrogation and review. VV admits to Ganapathi. "But my last dream, Ganapathi, leaves me with a far more severe problem. If it means anything, anything at all, it means that I have told my story so far from a completely mistaken perspective. I have thought about it, Ganapathi, and I realize I have no choice. I must retell it" (418).

If it is directly stated that the story has to be retold from the beginning, then the reader is left to wonder whether this perception of the past has also been a mistaken one. The implication is the difficulty/ impossibility of absolute judgment. The heroes of yesteryears could become villains of today and the villains of the past could become the martyrs of today. Since history is a matter of opinion, it can have only relative standards and never absolute standards.

Tharoor's novel itself is interpreted from various points of view, such as postmodernism, post-structuralism, postcolonialism and New Historicism. Sethuraman in 'Literature after Theory: A Case Study,' observing the indeterminacy principle present in the major theme(s) of the fictional work says, "My contention is that such a novel could only have been written after the deconstructive turn that rhetorical-critical disclosure has taken since Derrida" (130).

Critics have noticed postcolonial dimensions in Tharoor's novel. M.F. Salat says:

> In 'The Second Book' of the novel, Ved Vyas expresses his deeply felt anger at the school children's gross ignorance of Gangaji (alias Gandhiji) not long after his death and blames it on what he calls "the bastard educational institutions the British sired on us" (47). Although he does not dwell upon this aspect of the colonial impact on Indian culture, in his disaffection with the colonial inheritance, he typifies a commonly shared attitudinal pattern amongst postcolonial

> writers which constitutes a chief reason for the need felt by these writers to undo the documents of colonial heritage. (128)

Even the subtitles of Tharoor's eighteen books, according to Salat, are carefully chosen by the novelist to subvert the perception of history. He says, that the subtitles such as The Jewel in Crown, The Far Pavilion, Midnight's Children, A Passage to India and The Jungle Book are quite significant:

> It is significant to note that a majority of these works enshrine (mix) perception of India, written as they are from a predominantly colonial perspective. Tharoor's parodic inversion of these titles can, therefore, be said to constitute an implicit criticism of the inadequate portrayal of India by these writers and a justification for the need to reinvent India by un-inventing the India represented in such works. (131)

Similar opinion is expressed by Viney Kirpal who says, "*The Great Indian Novel* opposes English history and tells the story of India's colonization (and thereafter) from a perspective that decentres the colonizers and foregrounds Indians and Indian systems" (49).

The possibility of several readings to the novel itself is the best testimony to the plurality of significance emphasized by the novelist. Supriya Karunakaran says, "in this age of assassinations and earthquakes, of instability, insecurity and flux, one looks to writers like Vikram Seth and Shashi Tharoor who apparently challenge the system, but actually, infuse it with new life and vigour" (97).

Chapter III

Draupadi as the Archetypal Victim: Pratibha Ray's *Yajnaseni*

Pratibha Ray's *Yajnaseni* is a similar attempt at fictionalizing the epic from Draupadi's point of view. The epic plot of heroism starting with a seemingly simple tale of fraternal feud resulting in an archetypal war is transformed into a fictional autobiography of Draupadi. *Yajnaseni* can be considered an epistolary novel. The entire novel is one long letter written to her spiritual companion Krishna the Saki at the very end of her life. It narrates what happened to her as a woman, a wife and a mother. The other events of the *Mahabharata* revolve around the centre—the life and character of Draupadi. Even the major characters of the epic, particularly the male characters such as Bhishma, Yudhishthir and Dhritarashtra are marginalized to make Draupadi's life the centre of focus. The novelist, setting aside the chronological sequence of the events, selects only those that have a direct bearing on Draupadi's life.

The etymology of the several names by which she is known makes an interesting reading. She is Draupadi, as she is the daughter of the king Drupad. She is Panchali, the princes of Panchal. She is Yajnaseni as she is born from the sacrificial fires—the yajna, performed by her father Yajnasena. She is also known as Krishna—the dark complexioned.

The origin of the novel is traced back to an incident involving her name. A woman bearing the name of Krishna left her debauched, drunkard of a husband and went to live in her father's house. Remarriage was the only solution recommended by many of her sympathizers. She left for West Germany to stay with her brother. Later she is reported to have married a young man and had children. The novelist records with anguish the reaction of her sympathizers to the second marriage of Krishna "well when her very name is Krishna, she could be happy only after taking a second husband. Arreh, the Krishna of the *Mahabharata* took five husbands and still not being satisfied, was attracted to Karna and Krishna" (401).

Pratibha Ray says that the root of her sorrow were such thoughtless words against the devoted and powerful woman Krishnas of Dvaparayuga. "But how far do we know Krishna? How much knowledge do we have of the majesty of the *Mahabharata* and its noble culture?" (401), asks Ray. In her novel Ray reacts against the stigma attached to the name of Draupadi. In an interview given to Sue Dickman in *The Book Review* she states the reason for writing a novel to Draupadi. "What made me write on Draupadi and Ahalya? You may ask why I didn't write on Sita. Because these characters are eclipsed and misunderstood. I have always had a weakness towards a misunderstood group, misunderstood people" (33).

In *Yajnaseni*, the process of fictionalizing involves a reinterpretation of the character of Draupadi. The novelist introduces a transformation in the character brought about by suffering. She makes Draupadi a proponent of women's rights. Susan Bassnet and Harish Trivedi observe that the two great Indian epics are "worked and reworked by countless writers in Sanskrit as well as in all Indian languages with various shifts of emphasis and ideology through which gaps in the original were inventively filled in, silences were rendered poignantly articulate" (9). By adopting the first person narrative, Ray examines the female psyche of Draupadi and renders the suffering of all the women characters such as Satyavati, Amba, Madri, Gandhari and Uttara poignantly. Draupadi's spiritual intimacy with Krishna is reemphasized in the novel. The novelist retains the mythical accounts of her extraordinary birth and marriage. Some of the incidents chosen are true to Vyasa's epic. Vyasa's epic is only a record of events, it is not an interpretative exercise through probing the inner consciousness of the characters. But Pratibha Ray examines the psyche of Yajnaseni and records her reactions to certain incidents in her life. Such an imaginative perception of Draupadi's reaction to events makes the work distinctly fictional.

The narrative has unmistakable feminist overtones as Draupadi reflects on all the misery and agony she went through in her life. In "The Attitude of Modern Creative Writers towards the *Mahabharata*: Oriya Scene," J.M Mohanty remarks that the novel *Yajnaseni* shows a contemporary feminist attitude towards the great ancient epic (Dandekar 279). The novelist adapts the story of Yajnaseni to the contemporary situation deploring in no uncertain terms, social atrocities against women.

Yajnaseni places all her grievances on record in her letter to Krishna, written in the last moments of her life when she fell at the foot of the mount Himavant. It is very painful to her that none of her husbands turned back even to look. Rather Yudhishthir, the lord of righteousness, said to Bhim, "Do not turn back to look! Come forward" (3). Her fault, according to him, was her preference for Arjun.

In Vyasa's epic this incident is reported in Mahaprasthanika Parva 2.6 "Yudhishthir said: she had great partiality for Dhananjaya in particular. She obtains the fruit of that conduct today, O best of men" (Dutt 7:541).

Ray's novel imaginatively captures the reaction of Yajnaseni to these words of Yudhishthir. Shattered by the indifference of Yudhishthir, Yajnaseni regrets why she had to bear the burden of the whole world's mockery, sneers, innuendos, abuse, scorn and slander for the sake of preserving Yudhishthir's dharma (3). All along she had deluded herself of her husband's love and care. But such fond notions stood debunked in the end. She is afraid that her name will be object of derision and contempt:

> Draupadi will be food for mockery and jest amid the perverted sexuality of Kaliyuga's debauched men and women. How will these people appreciate that the five-husbanded Draupadi has to burn inch-by-inch in the cause of chastity? Then the heroine of Hastinapur, Draupadi, will become a condemned soul, the heroine of a tale of calumny. (3)

She lays bare the incidents of her life so that "the people of Kali-yuga will be able to decide whether the insults Draupadi suffered have been borne by any woman of any time" (4).

Pratibha Ray makes Yajnaseni a representative of Indian women in general who protest against discrimination and demand equality and gender justice. For Yajnaseni the most humiliating and agonizing moment in her life was when she was staked and lost by Yudhishthir in the game of dice. She protests against a woman being treated as "an object" or "the other."

> Full of anguish and anger I was thinking: was woman merely man's movable or immovable property? Was I part of Yudhishthir's movable or immovable property, male and female slaves, horses and elephants? Being a woman did I not have right even over myself, my own soul? If they had rights over this body of mine, did it mean they could do as they wished with me? (235)

Though the incident is true to Vyasa's epic, some of the issues raised by Pratibha Ray through Yajnaseni's protest in the novel are similar to the issues raised by western feminists. To see gender differences causing inequality between the sexes and such differences as the cultural constructs is a perception of the western feminists. An account of the western feminist perspective has been included in the first chapter. Simon de Beauvoir vehemently condemns discrimination against women based on gender differences. Yajnaseni's fury against the denial of basic rights to her as a human being strongly echoes Beauvoir's insistence that a woman be defined as a human being in quest of values.

True to the epic, Yajnaseni of Ray questions the propriety of the act of Yudhishthir. "Does even the most immoral uncivilized gambler ever stake his wife? Has any one ever done such a detestable act in the history of the world?" (234) When she demanded justice and asked the elders in the sabha whether her husband had got the right to stake her after he had already staked and lost his own self, every one was silent. Even Bhishma could not provide an answer to the perplexing question of Yajnaseni. Bhishma said "Immáculate one! One who is dependent does not have the right to stake someone else's wealth. But the wife is ever her husband's dependent. Therefore whether after having lost himself Yudhishthir has the right to stake you or not, is genuinely a dilemma" (35).

Draupadi raises this question of propriety in Vyasa's epic too. Bimal Krishna Matilal in *Moral Dilemmas in the Mahabharata* discusses the issue in an exclusive chapter. He says that the question raised by Draupadi remains unanswered and he presents four points for critical consideration from Vikarna's speech in defence of Draupadi:

1) The transaction took place at the instance of others, while Yudhishthira was engrossed totally in the vice of gambling. Therefore it was not valid.
2) Draupadi, being the wife of all the five Pandavas, Yudhishthira had no right to put her on stack (Sic). Hence, the act without proper authority could not be accepted.
3) Yudhishthira had himself lost first; therefore, he had no authority to stack Draupadi.
4) Initial idea and suggestion was that of Shakuni and not Yudhishthira. Hence, this was a fraudulent act and stood nullified (153).

He disputes three of the points and dismisses them as invalid because first of all, Yudhishthir could not be called an addict, secondly, the other Pandavas did not question the authority of Yudhishthir and, thirdly, Yudhishthir did not complain of a fraudulent act by Shakuni. Only the question of the authority of the husband over his wife needs to be considered. What Bhishma meant by husband's dependent has to be comprehended in the light of the socio-cultural norms of that society. In the ancient society the wife was dependent on her husband for her protection. The novel contains a reference to the cult of husband-worshipping by ancient Indian women. "The husband was the wife's God. If he was unable to protect his wife then how could he be God? Only the man who could protect, could be God. Therefore placing Krishna on God's pedestal I used to worship him. It was he, who was my friend in danger, my savior" (38).

Yudhishthir not only failed to protect the honour of his wife, but also was instrumental in bringing about her dishonor. Hence

Yajnaseni furiously denounces her husband for his gross misdeed. She affirms: "the destruction of the country where men do not rise to protect the honour of women is inevitable" (249). This utterance is a veritable truth in the history of the world as witnessed and borne out in the case of Troy, Lanka and Madura. Yajnaseni's protest is powerfully brought out in her letter to Krishna. Strategically, the letter is a kind of an interior monologue revealing her inner agony. The denunciation of her husband is alien to the character of Vyasa's Draupadi. In the epic the question raised by Draupadi is clever argument regarding the legality of Yudhishthir's stake. The intention is to extricate herself and her husbands from the disgraceful situation by debating about the legitimacy of the stake. Irawati Karve remarks that loyalty to her husbands is one of the distinguishing virtues of the epic heroine.

> The Draupadi of the *Mahabharata* stormed and raged; but to the last moment she remained a faithful wife. There is not a single incident in her life that casts the slightest suspicion on her life. [. . .] Her sensitive pride, her willingness to sacrifice and her faithfulness to her husbands were the qualities appropriate to her country, time and clan; she was extraordinary but this extraordinariness was born out of the ordinary values of her time. (95-97)

Such is the plight of the heroines of the Indian epics. Pratibha Ray in "The Real and the Spiritual," an interview given to Ranavir Ranga in the *Indian Literature* says: 'oppression and exploitation of women in a male dominated or patriarchal society has been the prime theme of the two epics of the world, the *Ramayana* and the *Mahabharata*" (129). In the novel Yajnaseni emerges as the archetypal victim, a much wronged woman. She identifies herself with Satyavati, Amba and also with the Sita and *Ramayana*. "The supremely wise mother Satyavati had to suffer the scorn and mockery of society sometimes because of her past. But Parashar? He was respected by all. [. . .] But faultless Amba was rejected by the narrow-minded king Shalva. What was her offence?" (95)

But the epic does not give an impression that Satyavati had to suffer shame or ignominy on account of her past. Whereas Kunti could not reveal to anyone the birth of her son outside wedlock due to fear and shame, Satyavati could boldly reveal to Bhishma the existence of her son born outside wedlock fathered by Parashar. Parashar and Shalva have not been accused of causing injustice to women, according to traditional sentiments. But Bhishma has been condemned by feminists and non-feminists alike for being unfair to most women in the epic such as Amba, Gandhari, Madri and Draupadi. Though taking a feminist stance in her novel, Pratibha Ray refrains from accusing Bhishma of injustice to women. This is in keeping with the tradition of holding Bhishma in high esteem.

According to Ray's Yajnaseni, the beginning of her suffering can be traced back to her polyandrous marriage to the Pandava brothers. The predicament of having to marry five men baffled her. "My mind rebelled. Did I have no say? Then what was the meaning of Svayamwar?" (56) She could look upon only Arjun as her husband. But she was furious on finding him totally unheroic when he did not rebel on hearing that his bride was to be turned into an object of enjoyment for his elder and younger brothers.

Ray views the situation from a twentieth century perspective. In the novel Yajnaseni questions the denial of individual freedom which is the fundamental right of a human being. She voices the sentiments of the women of today who insist on their consent and decision to be honoured in the choice of a husband. Such a demand is in keeping with the growing awareness of the need to alleviate the suffering of women due to forced marriages.

Introducing an element of dilemma in Yajnaseni's mind, Pratibha Ray dramatizes the situation. Draupadi could not accept Arjun's brothers also as her husbands as she considered the one who won her in the Svayamwar only, as her husband. She thought that her very name would become a stigma as the world would condemn her as a despicable and stained character. "To sacrifice myself for safeguarding the dharma of others—was that my duty or was it my duty to choose one husband for the sake of my self-respect and happiness? This I could not make out?" (59) Yajnaseni feels that her situation is far worse than that of the Sita of the *Ramayana*:

> Chaste Sita did not have to face such a situation, then for preserving unity among Ram, Lakshman, Bharat and Shatrughana. Sita did not have to marry all the four brothers. Despite not getting Sita as their wife, Lakshman, Bharat and Shatrughana had remained loyal brothers of Ram. Why would the five Pandava brothers not remain loyal to one another without me? (62)

Pratibha Ray makes Draupadi accept the proposal on the ground that the interest of the family is regarded by the heroine herself as far more important than the interest of self. Seetha Srinivasan in "In Search of an Identity" says that "the Indian social landscape believes in the security and stability of marriage even while (paradoxically) permitting every kind of deviant behaviour in man-woman relationship" (1+) Secondly, Yajnaseni receives a hint to this effect from Krishna who is her soul companion.

In Vyasa's epic there is no direct reaction from Draupadi. But her father Drupad expresses his shock. Yudhishthir quotes precedents from the past—that of Jatila who married seven sages, and that of Varkshi who married ten brothers known as Pracetases. In the end, Vyasa becomes the arbiter of the dispute. He pronounces the judgement that what Yudhishthira says is not censurable and that Draupadi is ordained to be the wife of five husbands. In Adi Parva 197.35-49 Vyasa gives a mythical explanation of how such a marriage has been preordained. The mythical account narrates how Indra as a penalty for having insulted Siva is divided into five parts and born on the earth as Pandavas. Similarly the daughter of a sage who asked Siva five times for a husband was granted the wish. She is born as Yajnaseni and gets five husbands true to the mythical report. There is a significant silence in Vyasa's epic about the reaction of Draupadi to such a proposal. Such silences are exploited by the novelist in her depiction of the character of Draupadi. To portray Yajnaseni agitated and torn between the interests of the self and the family will carry conviction among her readers.

Ray also presents her heroine Yajnaseni as being very suspicious of Kunti's intentions. 'Even though she had sons through different gods at her husband's interest [. . .]. In case the mother was shamed before her daughter-in-law and looked small, she had deliberately compelled the daughter-in-law to accept five husbands' (66).

Draupadi's doubts about Kunti's intentions are a fictional twist in the novel. This may be true in the Indian context where sometimes the problems faced by women are created by women themselves. The woman-against-woman syndrome is one of the ills of the Indian society, where the joint family system is still in vogue.

The acceptance of a strange situation should not be misconstrued as acceptance of an immoral or sinful living, as Draupadi felt that greater good lay in her duty to others. Ray's heroine revolts against making a mockery of her polyandrous marriage. She questions the application of double standards of morality to men and women. Ray refers to a visitor from the abode of the gods who questioned Govind about the propriety of a woman marrying five men; Yajnaseni's reaction is one of fury:

> She stood up in revolt against the law of the abode of the gods, according to which, one man might accept as many women as he wished, but if one woman married more than one husband she would be branded a sinner. Who had laid down this law? It must be some male god! Otherwise how could there be such a distinction of virtue and sin between male and female? All the rituals and rules that had been created in society built around the distinction between rich-poor, high-low, Brahmin-chandal, male-female, and such others, the profound inequities that had been set up based upon consideration of virtue and sin—against all of these, a life-long war would have to be waged. (92)

The novelist's concern about wiping out social inequality is also evident here. Discrimination based on gender differences should be deplored. "I would get angry, 'Chaste woman! Unchaste woman! In the same way why don't the scriptures speak of chaste men and unchaste men? Are men's hearts made of gold that sin cannot tarnish them? Have the scriptures, prescribed lists of sins only for women?'" (94)

Yajnaseni's fury against male chauvinism is a common reaction of the feminists. Her fears come true when Karna calls her an unchaste woman in Vyasa's epic at the time of her disrobing in the

Kuru Sabha. Whether Karna means it seriously or he is trying to settle an old score with her is yet another question. Karna-Draupadi relationship as portrayed in the novel is dealt with, later in this chapter.

Yajnaseni's comparison of her suffering with that of Sita of *Ramayana* goes to prove the fact that the Indian literary tradition highlights the dilemma of women—heroic women, mythical or real. Sita, Savitri, Vasuki and Kannagi have all been venerated and defied as Goddesses of chastity. They continue to hold sway over the minds of the creative writers. Madhu Kishwar in "Yes to Sita, No to Ram" says that "the injustice done to Sita seems to weigh very heavily on the collective conscience of men in India" (242). Sita's suffering and Draupadi's sufferings are different kinds of suffering. Sita did not have to face the dilemma of discrimination against women. The births of Sita and Yajnaseni have been extraordinary phenomena. Both grew up as princesses; both had to live in the forests for years after their marriages.

In spite of these similarities, the overall impact is one of contrast. Whereas Sita's life in the forest was caused by Rama's idealism, Draupadi's life in the forest was caused by Yudhishthir's addiction to gambling. It is a common sentiment among Indian women that the ideals set in bygone ages by the epic heroines such as Savithri and Sita are still valid and worth emulating. Writers such as Madhu Kishwar comment on the contrast between Sita and Draupadi:

> Sita's offer of *agnipariksha* and her coming out of it unscathed is by and large seen not as an act of supine surrender to the whims of an unreasonable husband but as an act of defiance that challenges her husband's aspersions as a means of showing him to be so flawed in his judgement that the gods have to come and pull up Ram for his foolishness. Unlike Draupadi, she does not call upon them for help. Their help comes unsolicited. (24)

True to Vyasa's epic, Ray's Yajnaseni also appealed to the gods to save her honour; but she was driven to such extreme humiliation when her husbands remained mute spectators to the atrocious act of Dushasana. Karve remarks, "Two words keep recurring in reference to Draupadi—'nathavati anathavat' (having husbands, but like a widow). She was the wife of the five but bereft, the daughter of a rich house but like an orphan, she had brave allies but she was alone. This was the pity of her situation." (91) Yajnaseni describes her situation poignantly: "how terrifyingly helpless I felt! Who will understand that? I do not know where Bhim and Arjun's prowess and valour disappeared. Yudhishthir's humility and devotion to dharma—is that what it was? The destruction of the country where men do not rise to protect the honour of women is inevitable (249).

The novelist seems to put forth a plea for uniform standards of virtue and sin for both men and women. Such a plea is similar to the vociferous demand of many a contemporary feminist:

> Yet Ambika and Ambalika had to bear the brunt of mockery on several occasions. For having becoming (sic) pregnant by another man they had to suffer social odium; when Kunthi, bowing to her husband's commands gave birth to sons by various gods, she too was insulted several times because of this. Thinking over all these incidents it seems that if the standards of virtue and sin had been identical for women and men, the female race would not have been oppressed by social tyranny. (97)

It has been already pointed out that 'Niyoga' was an accepted custom, according to the social norms of the ancient times, and it was not condemned as a deviant behaviour or an immoral act in that society. Ray here applies the contemporary standards of morality to the practices of an earlier epoch. It is not always possible to judge the past by the present standards.

By and large the novelist has preserved the traditional image of Draupadi as a forceful personality—able, brave and beautiful but revengeful. But Yajnaseni's call for revenge and deterrent punishment for crimes against women is a protest against injustice. Vyasa's epic heroine is a consistent personality confident of her strength of mind and will power. She remained unflinching in her determination of refusal to compromise with the wicked. Her exile and suffering could never blunt her purpose. In the Udyoga Parva ch. 82 of Vyasa, there is an account of how Draupadi insisted on retributive punishment. When Krishna decides to go on a peace mission to the Kauravas on the eve of war, Draupadi reminds him of the humiliation she received at the hand of the Kauravas.

In Vyasa's epic itself, the war is seen as a war against injustice to women. It is the oppression of women that is foregrounded by Pratibha Ray in her novel. The contemporary relevance of the epic lies in the fact that it has taken up the cause of women as an oppressed group thousands of years ago. In Ray's novel Krishna tells Draupadi, "After your insult in the Kuru court, this earth cannot be saved from a great war" (252). Draupadi of the epic, in fact, can be considered as the founding mother of feminists all over the world as she did not let the injustice done to her go unavenged. Ray's Yajnaseni asserts the moral strength of women:

> Tolerance is the ornament of women. But to bear injustice with bowed head is not the dharma of women. [. . .] The remaining days of my life I will fight against injustice, adharma, sin [. . .] though the world may call me an ogress because of this, the world must know that the woman, who creates, is auspicious, is also the destroyer of the sinful and the wicked. It is after washing my hair in Dushasana's blood that I shall tie it up. Dushasana who, regarding women as weak, dragged me by the hair and insulted me. Then will the world know that while woman's heart is delicate, it is not weak. (251)

When Jayadrath assaulted her, Yajnaseni insisted on nothing but death penalty for him and Bhim was her sole protector. But Yudhishthir began to explain the nobility of forgiving. Ray's Yajnaseni flared up in fury saying, "the working of our society is such that throughout life a woman has to suffer because of sin" (321). She calls for some radical changes in the outlook of the society and some deterrent punishment for crimes against women:

> If the desire for another's wife were an unpardonable crime and shameful for man, then there would not be so much of sin and perversion in the world. Chaste Sita's life too would not have been so sorrowful. After the killing of Ravan and the destruction of Lanka, rape and beastly tyranny would have vanished from earth. For men, women have also become something to be won like kingdom, wealth and prosperity. He whose might is greater, wins the wives of others. [. . .] I pardoned Jayadrath but began cursing womanhood for the inequality in the rules and laws of society for the sexes. (322)

Yajnaseni's protest against different set of rules for the sexes is similar to the views of Kate Millett and Simon de Beauvoir who vehemently oppose the criterion of sexual differences for treatment of women. Yajnaseni finds crimes against women rampant. She warns the society that if those who were responsible for the horrifying outrage that she suffered in the court were let unpunished, then "the history of Bharata will be filled with shameful accounts of atrocities against women" (251).

Ray emphasizes the point that the epic has set up a precedent for real rehabilitation of destitute women. Krishna has displayed exemplary conduct in liberating women from oppression and tyranny. This is well illustrated in the incident of Krishna rescuing women from the tyranny of Narakasura; but the problem did not stop with putting an end to his tyranny. The rescued women were not accepted by their parents. Rather they sent messages: "Suicide is the only path open. After so many days in the custody of Narakasur, no prince—not even the humblest man—will take their hand in marriage" (152). Then Krishna felt that it was his duty to accept them as his wives to give them social security:

> By this the world's male society would realize that it is not the body of woman that was the woman; that the woman has a soul too. Though imprisoned in the body the soul does not become a prisoner. Even if the body is thrown into stinking hell its sin does not rub off on the soul. [. . .] I have respected the immaculate souls of these thousand princesses, married them, accepted them. [. . .] Those who cannot understand the nature of my love call me a debauch. (153)

Such a nobility of purpose is not explicitly stated in the epic of Vyasa. Ray's reinterpretation of Draupadi's character involves some deviations from the epic of Vyasa. For instance, the relationship between Karna and Draupadi has been altered by Ray. In Vyasa's epic the relationship between the two is marked by bitterness and mutual animosity. Karna has been gnawing within from the insult hurled at him during Draupadi's Svayamwar. She rejects him on account of being a charioteer's son and a non-Kshatriya. This marks the beginning of the soured relationship between the two. Karna avenges this insult at the time of her disrobing. He encourages Dushasana to strip her off in the Sabha and calls her an unchaste woman. In the novel Ray modifies the relationship between the two. She makes Dhristadyumna rather than his sister leading the humiliation of Karna in Draupadi's Svayamwar. He questions the right of Karna to participate in the Svayamwar. "Unless the suitor is high born, my sister cannot wed him. However great a hero Karna, the son of a charioteer Adirath and Radha might be, he cannot have the right to win my sister" (42).

Yajnaseni's reaction to the rebuff of Karna is one of sympathy. She says, "my heart was full of remorse, particularly because Karna had been insulted by raising the question of his birth. In truth what was the necessity for this Svayamwar?" (42) She hears a sad tune playing in the secret crevice of her heart from time to time for Karna (279). She even goes to the extent of seeking his forgiveness, saying, "for the mistake committed by my brother in the Svayamwar hall because of which you have suffered insult and humiliation, as your daughter-in-law I crave forgiveness" (364).

Equally remorse-stricken is Karna for treating her unkindly. When Krishna discloses to him that the Pandavas are his younger brothers, he says, "As the wife of my younger brothers, she is like my daughter-in-law. And yet I led the onslaught on her modesty and honour, for that I beg forgiveness from you" (352).

Ray has also made an addition to the epic of Vyasa by describing an incident of Karna rescuing Draupadi from the river Yamuna in spate. Such an incident, absent from the original epic, is introduced by Ray to project Karna-Draupadi relationship as one of cordiality and mutual sympathy.

A similar fictional twist has been given by P.K. Balakrishnan in his novel *Eni Njan Urangatte* (Now let me sleep) written in Malayalam. This novel is also a fictional rendering of the epic from Draupadi's point of view. In a review of the novel, in *New Quest*, Jancy James refers to this aspect: "the most striking feature of *Eni Njan Urangatte* is this sympathetic insight into the character of Karna traced through the stream of Draupadi's consciousness" (93).

Forgiveness is certainly not one of the virtues of the epic heroine who never hesitated to wreak appalling vengeance on those who wronged her. "Beauty and imperious pride must have made an overwhelming combination in Draupadi," according to Krishna Chaitanya (147). Ray, perhaps, has altered the version of the original to invest Draupadi with exceptional nobility. There are other instances also in the novel which seem to project a different image of Draupadi. Contrary to the picture of Vyasa's epic, Pratibha Ray portrays her as one who strove for universal brotherhood and racial amity. In the novel Yajnaseni emphasizes the need for integration of the Aryans and Non-Aryans. She puts forth a powerful plea for "construction of roads linking the forest of Kamyak, Dvaita, Naimesha and different places of the Himalayas, the Ashrams of sages and Hastinapur" (299). She wishes to use her ornaments for the sacred task of establishing amity on earth (361).

In yet another situation when Bhim is about to strike a mortal blow to Kirmir, she pleads with him to spare him. "By saving Kirmir we might be able to build a bridge of amity between Kirats and Pandavas," says Yudhishthir, endorsing the view of Draupadi.

In Vyasa's' epic, the image of Draupadi as a wife dominates her image as a mother. But in Ray's novel, Draupadi as a mother is projected with equal emphasis. Seeing the twin sons of Virat, Kambu and Jambu crying in hunger, Yajnaseni starts feeding them. She says: "Aryans and Non-Aryans are distinctions made by men. The blood of all is the same. Mother's milk is the same for all. Give me the chance to earn merit" (271). Referring to the depiction of Draupadi as bringing about the Arya-Anarya harmony, Pratibha Ray in "Voice of the Voiceless," an interview given to Sathi, says, "Any kind of discrimination—colour, race, region, sex, economics—between human beings pains me" (87). In this context it is appropriate to consider the views of the present-day historians who dismiss the theory of Aryan invasion as a myth.

Such powerful utterance by Draupadi promoting the cause of racial amity runs contrary to the spirit of the original. The proud and vengeful heroine of Vyasa is made to play the role of a social reformer in the 20th century striving hard to wipe out racial discrimination. In the novel Yudhishthir says, "I thought that princess Draupadi's burning character was filled with anger, pride, revenge only. But now I have understood how much of humanity and superhuman quality permeates it" (301).

Such deviations seem to have some significance in the context of the twentieth century. Several writers are engaged in the task of raising the consciousness of the public as well as the rulers to the plight of the tribals. Social revolutions have been effectively brought about by writers in the history of the world. The contribution of Voltaire and Rousseau to the rise of French Revolution is an undisputable fact. Pratibha Ray seems to be a committed artist. She has concentrated on giving a vivid picture of the lives of the Bonda tribes in Orissa in her writings. In an interview given to Ranavir Ranga, Ray admits that she reinterpreted the character of Draupadi keeping in mind the present state of the world:

> My Draupadi has throughout pleaded for the welfare of mankind and raised her voice against moral decay and degeneration of personal honesty of Kauravas, Jayadratha and ethical norms in social life. Even if experiencing great personal tragedy, suffering, exploitation, humiliation and various kinds of social decay, she has always pleaded for emotional integration peace and harmony in the universe. She has taken bold steps against social evils like casteism, trying to bring the underprivileged into the mainstream. All these in my opinion are reinterpretations of the past keeping in view the present state of the world. My Draupadi is a social reformer begging rebirth to serve her nation again and again dreaming for a nuclear—free civilization. (131)

The transformation of the character of Draupadi seems to be a meaningful change, indeed in a society with its changing perspectives to suit the needs of the time. Ray makes no secret of her ambition as a writer. In an interview given to Sivasankari in *Knit India through Literature: The East*, Pratibha Ray says, "It is my ambition to see humanity lead a meaningful life. As a writer, I want to sow the seeds for social growth and progressive thought through my writings" (342).

To this avowed aim of promoting social reform, Ray has adapted the myths found in the original. The extraordinariness of her heroine has been explained in terms of a mythical account of her birth and her marriage to the Pandavas. There are several other myths also resurging in her novel. The novel highlights Yajnaseni's love for Krishna. The relationship is by no means amorous but spiritual. In accordance with the Bhakti-cult in India, Draupadi looks upon Krishna as her lover, as her sole protector and her only refuge. "I was lost in a dream—Krishna's form. That vision was my constant companion." (11) She wanted to garland Krishna but the appearances created an illusion. She says, "the garland I had been weaving since the morning to put round Krishna's neck would have to be put round Arjun's" (23). Viewed against the mythical background, Arjun seems to be another half of Krishna. "Arjun is after all my alter ego," says Krishna (207).

The miracle of Draupadi blessed with infinite length of cloth when Dushasana tried to disrobe her is interpreted on an ethical plane as the act of one good deed generating another. When Krishna's Sudarshan Chakra cut his finger during Shishupal-vadha it is said that Yajnaseni tore off her auspicious sari to put a bandage around the injured finger. Krishna seems to have returned this debt of her kindness at the time of her humiliation.

Pratibha Ray strangely feels that myths provide patterns of exemplary behaviour and ethical values. In an interview with the novelist, Ranavir Ranga draws her attention to the view that the modern mind fails to grasp many a myth such as those connected with Draupadi Chiraharana, Vishwarupa and so on hailed in our great epic *Mahabharata*, dismissing them as unbelievable in this age of science. She explains the function of myths in her works:

> My effort in Yajnaseni was to fight against the system which believes in the power of Demon which spread like fire, violence, hatred and inhumanity and believes the supernatural power dismissing myths as Mithya. Therefore, I did not endeavour to deviate from the original the incidents of Draupadi's life and allowed the already spoon-fed modern mind to give an insight into human life. [. . .] That the blending of spiritual authority with man's will power can save him from a great calamity has been symbolized by Draupadi's Vastraharana. [. . .] Reinterpretation of the past for the benefit of the present for me is not attaching scientific reasons to incidents but inculcating human values through reinterpretation of the characters. (134)

Towards the end of the novel, the transformation of the character becomes complete. Yajnaseni advocates peace and harmony by a strong denunciation of war, strife and disintegration. She puts forth a prayer to Krishna that whatever had happened to her should not happen to any other woman:

> Lay down a rule that no woman will ever have several husbands at a time. Keeping myself indivisible the pain of being divided is known to me. The second thing compassionate Krishna! Do not let even the enemy grieve for his sons. There is no grief in the world greater than this. [. . .] The third thing the pain that I suffered in the court. Let no other woman in the world ever have to go through this. [. . .] The fourth thing that I ask is for this world. I request that because of race, religion, language and colour let no country split into parts like Hastina and Indraprastha. Inequality is the variety of your creation. Let not the integrity, unity and purity of any country be destroyed. (396)

The feminist views expressed in Pratibha Ray's novel need a careful examination. Feminism as seen in Ray's novel is not a passionate advocating of female superiority in all spheres of life; but an awareness of the identity of woman and her strengths. While speaking up for Yajnaseni, the novelist attempts to dispel certain popular misconceptions about women, which are the cultural constructs of a society entrenched in patriarchy. The woman is looked upon as 'the other,' the weaker sex in relation to man; she is always dependent on man, denied education and equal opportunities.

Such patriarchal notions are the impact of colonial legacy in India. Indian tradition has always looked upon woman as 'Shakthi' or the Embodiment of cosmic energy. The novel to a certain extent is a record of the real strength of women who can bear several onslaughts on her mind and body; but nothing can cow down her spirit, and her indomitable will. "Any woman irrespective of age, cast and religion and country is worthy of a man's respect. For, a woman is formed of Shakthi and without worshipping Shakthi none can become a hero" (45).

In the novel Shakuni and Karna are presented as representatives of the patriarchal society. Shakuni denies the privilege of learning to women. "The greatest offence a woman commits is to try to be learned. It is because she became wise and scholarly that her condition is thus. If she had grovelled at our feet and begged, perhaps, she might have escaped such a gross insult. Just as knowledge and power enhance a man's attraction, similarly ignorance and helplessness increase the charm of a woman" (238). Karna remarks, "Where there is a woman there is hell" (304).

The statement of Shakuni and Karna viewed from the twentieth century perspective would provoke loud protests from women; for in the context of growing awareness about the status of women, education is the chief means of empowerment of women. But neither an ancient woman nor an emancipated woman of the twentieth century would agree that ignorance and helplessness increase the charm of a woman. Even Bhima shares the opinion of Shakuni. "What is the use of women being learned?" (76) He sounds like a male chauvinist when he declares, "Let them be good cooks, provide service, laugh with me, talk to me, sing to me, do whatever I command instantly" (76).

Women are not mere objects of man's pleasure. Ray observes in "A Writer's Pain and Pleasure—Some Meandering Reflections": "the principled domineering type of brilliant and gifted women are considered unwomanly according to the age-old double standard norm of the society" (150). Both history and mythology give ample proof of brave intelligent women in India. Even in the ancient Vedic society, there were women scholars such as Gargi, Lopamudra and Maitreyi. P. Thomas in *Ancient Indian Feminists* refers to the existence of several spirited women in different ages of Indian history who have asserted their individuality:

> Panchali virtually ruled over her husbands. Kumaradevi wife of Chandra Gupta [. . .] was termed Mahadevi—the great queen—and even coins were minted in her name, a privilege accorded only to kings. Again Mrinal Devi, mother of the great Sidharaj Jayasingh, ruled over Gujarat at the end of the eleventh century. Rani Durgavati, the Rathod queen of Jodhpur had not only to rule the state for her infant son but had to defend it against the Great Moghul Aurangzeb. Coming to more recent times Ahalya Bai Holkar of Indore was an illustrious woman who ruled on behalf of her adopted son. Rani of Jhansi took active part in the Great Mutiny. (275)

Yajnaseni is portrayed as a victim of patriarchal society. The predicament of Indian women entrenched in patriarchal society is identical with that of the western women. But there are basic differences in the value systems and ethos of these two societies.

Madhu Kishwar's "A Horror of Isms: Why I do not call Myself a Feminist" provides great insights into the position of women in India. She analyses the basic differences between Indian and Western feminism.

> Feminism in the west emerged as a powerful challenge to existing power structures and gender equations at the level of the family, the economy and the polity. When used in the Western context, the word 'feminism' evokes many positive associations of nearly two centuries or more of struggle by courageous women who braved social attack, ridicule ostracism and male wrath in order to press women's claim for equality at home and in the workplace. (276)

Madhu Kishwar says that the word feminism evokes no such positive connotations in India. The idea of women's rights and dignity is not alien to our society. Truly, she avers that we have a much longer history of individual women's assertiveness in India and a well-established tradition of making space for women whose aspirations take them in directions different from the stereotypical in the Indian society. In the novel also, this view is re-emphasized by Pratibha Ray. Madhu Kishwar says that this tradition of Shaki cult allows "Indian society to be far more receptive to women's assertions and strengths, even while it practises very offensive forms of discrimination against women. [. . .] The nature and character of women's problems and their chosen methods of struggle remained substantially different from those of the Western feminist movements" (276).

Though Indian women are affected by the feminist rhetoric of the west, a large section of women seem to diverge from it. Suma Chitnis in "Feminism: Indian Ethos and Indian convictions" brings out three specific points on which the perceptions and sentiments of a large number of women differ from those of western feminists. She says that the average Indian woman disapproves of feminist anger. She observes that there is a confused reaction to feminists' emphasis on patriarchy and particularly on men as the principal oppressors. They are unable to tune into the demands of equality and personal freedom (Ghadially 82).

In the west, the claim to equality is one of the core principles of the political philosophy of many countries; but, in practice, women are never accepted as equals. "Under the circumstances, feminist anger in the west may be seen as women's cry against the hypocrisy of a culture that accords centrality to the values of equality and individual freedom but nevertheless denies equality to women" (Ghadially 83).

The causes for the mixed response of Indian women to western feminism, according to Chitnis, can be traced back to the social structure in India. Indian society has always been highly hierarchical. The factors that condition hierarchy are age, sex and position in the family. In the community, factors such as caste, lineage, learning, wealth and occupation determine hierarchy. The harshness and oppressiveness of all those hierarchies is somewhat relieved by a strong sense of defence to superiors, a sense of mutuality, a series of behavioural codes which bend superiors to fulfill their obligations to their inferiors and above all by a philosophy of self-denial and the cultural emphasis on sublimating the ego.

The essential outlook of the Indian woman is spelt out by Chitnis:

> The concept of equality as a correlate of the concept of individual freedom is alien to Indian society. It was first introduced into Indian culture through western education and through the exposure of western educated Indians to liberalism, at the beginning of the nineteenth century. But it did not have to bear the kind of injustices the women in the west had to suffer because of the continuing gap between political ideals and realities. (Ghadially 84)

Far from being oppressors, Indian men have taken pioneering efforts to enhance the status of women. It is a distinctive character of Indian society that social reforms to improve the conditions of women have been initiated by more men than women. Rajarammohun Roy's struggle for abolition of Sati marks the beginning of social awakening in India. Many others, especially men, championed the cause of women, such as Ishwar Chandra Vidyasagar, Keshav Chandra Sen, Malabari, Phule, Agarkar, Ranade and Karve. They took great efforts to abolish Sati, child marriages, the disfiguring of widows, the ban on the remarriage of upper caste Hindu windows and a host of other evil practices that affected women. They also worked hard to enhance the status of women by obtaining for them legal rights to property and by requiring the law to take cognizance of their status by providing them with some basic rights in matters such as adoption.

Some of the social reformers were staunch nationalists too. Their vision of independent India envisages a new society which enhances the status of women in India, accepting the concept of equality for women. The country's greatest leader Gandhiji also strove hard to communicate to the masses the concept of stree shakti, a positive tenet of the Hindu religion. Suma Chitnis comments on the principle of equality between the sexes in the Hindu religion:

> If Gandhi could communicate the concept of Stree Shakti (the moral power of womanhood) to the Indian masses so convincingly, it was because the Hindu religion carried a highly positive concept of the feminine principle. Unlike Christianity, Judaism, or Islam the image of God in Hinduism is not exclusively male. The female principle complements and completes the male. (Ghadially 87)

The concept of Ardhanareeshwara has been enshrined in the Hindu religion to underline the idea that the male and the female cannot be separated. The Vedas also say that the male is one half of the human body, the female the other half. A man cannot perform religious duties without the participation of his wife. Lord Shiva is adored by women as He is the embodiment of the feminist principle of equality allowing his spouse an important role in influencing his decision. Both tradition and history have affirmed the principle of equality. The ideals cherished by the Indian women are different from those of the western women: Pratibha Ray's Yajnaseni cannot be identified with western feminists. She is a typical Indian woman who wants, "only a life of peace and quiet, a world filled with husband and children [. . .] which is every woman's desire—not a jot more than that" (148).

The Indian women attach great value to the security and stability of marriage. The interest of the family is far more important to an Indian woman than the interest of the self. Self effacement is a precious value in view of the unity of the family. The Indian social landscape presents an ideal picture. Though there is hierarchy in the husband-wife relationship, there is mutual dependence and clear role definitions that avoid conflict in everyday life. One must also remember that if there was a code of conduct prescribed for the woman, there was a code of conduct prescribed for the man, too, which was eminently suitable for an agrarian society. It is only with the coming up of industrialization that a redefinition of roles has been necessitated, even in the west.

In any age, there is a gap between the ideal and reality. One must admit that in the Indian value system, the position of woman is one of respectability. But the contemporary reality is far from being desirable. There is adequate painful evidence of inferior status of women, sati, child marriage, polygamy, dowry-system, bride-burning and female infanticide. With the advancement of science and technology, sex-determination tests facilitate the cruelty of female infanticide. Thus in spite of constitutional and legal protection and a glorious tradition of Shakti Cult, women continue to suffer.

Pratibha Ray tries to bridge the gap between the ideal and reality by making Draupadi herself work towards social reform. The novelist's own sense of commitment to the society, particularly her concern for the tribals as an oppressed group, has influenced her depiction of Draupadi as a social reformer. Epic heroines such as Sita, Savitri and Draupadi have always inspired Indian women as archetypes and these ideal models still influence the lives of Indian women. It suits the purpose of Ray to make Draupadi herself a pacifist and a reformer.

Pratibha Ray is not the only writer to have projected Draupadi as the champion of the oppressed. Bharati, a Tamil poet, has portrayed Draupadi as a symbol of Indian womanhood. Referring to the vow Draupadi made in the Kuru Sabha, Prema Nandakumar says that it was meant to change Indian women with self-confidence and daring to defy the moribund, the obscurantist and dumb traditionalists who kept them bound within darkened rooms (19).

Mahasweta Devi's short story, "Dopdi" (Draupadi) is an attempt at deconstructing the epic heroine from the mythic lore and views her as a victim of social, material, racial and sexual conditions. The account of Draupadi's polyandrous marriage and the incident of her disrobing in the Kuru Sabha find ironic echoes in the story. Dopdi, the tribal woman, has been subjected to the tyranny and oppression of the higher class. She is the victim of a gang-rape. Mahasweta Devi's genuine concern about the lives of the tribal society in Bengal makes her rewrite the story of Draupadi. In "Dopdi," the binary opposition between the victor-victim is reversed. The villain Senanayak successfully strips her off. But the victim challenges him to clothe her by parading naked before him.

Commenting on the significance of the story Gayatri Chakravorty Spivak in her preface to her translation of the story in *Writing and Sexual Difference* says that the modern Dopdi is as heroic as Draupadi of the epic:

> It would be a mistake, I think, to read the modern story as a refutation of the ancient Dopdi as (heroic as) Draupadi. She is also what Draupadi—written into the patriarchal and authoritative sacred text as proof of male power—could not be. Dopdi is at once a palimpsest and a contradiction. (Abel 268)

The problems faced by women in India are seen as problems of the oppressed group. The novelist in the interview given to Sue Dickman clarifies that one who fights for the rights of women need not be branded as a feminist or as an enemy of men.

> You are fighting for women's rights as human beings. You should fight for human rights hand in hand with men. Men are not your enemies. Men are in society with you. You cannot create an earth full of women. You cannot create separate worlds for women and men. [. . .] Men can create many things—missiles and other things but they cannot preserve the culture. Through the world women have preserved culture. [. . .] Writers are sensitive towards problems around them, social problems. There are more problems for women around us; and those problems are more intense than men's problems. Therefore, as a writer, the intense problems attracted me, not as a woman's problem. (32)

Obviously feminist issues are emerging as larger issues of human rights, in India. Towards this effect Ray has worked, foregrounding the predicament of Draupadi.

Chapter IV

Challenging the Archetypes: Bhyrappa's *Parva*

S.L. Bhyrappa's *Parva* is a fictional rendering of the *Mahabharata* from the twentieth century perspective. In "*Mahabharata*: My Attempt at Recreation" the novelist says that he wants to understand the epic with his twentieth century mind (Dandekar 264). The twentieth century perspective is suggestive of a gamut of changes in the social, cultural, political and intellectual spheres of life. The rapid strides of progress in western science and technology have made man question the irrationalities of myth and religion. Feminism as a strong socio-political movement has brought about a number of changes in the developed countries and has not been without an effect in the developing countries. Social reawakening leads to the need for establishing gender justice and equality between the sexes. Several writers reassess the earlier works in view of the growing awareness about the status of women. The contemporary writers too cannot ignore the social realities of the times.

Bhyrappa affirms that he decided to see the whole material of the *Mahabharata* through the form of a novel (Dandekar 265). But irrespective of cultural and linguistic limitations, the novel, viewed as a fictional creation, gives infinite scope for the free play for the artist's imagination.

In *Parva* Bhyrappa combines several strategies in fictionalizing the epic. The process includes recasting of select events, reinterpretation of some characters, demythologization and distortion of myths resulting in startling deviations from the epic of Vyasa. The novelist demythologizes events such as the birth of Karna, the Pandavas and the Kauravas, the disrobing of Draupadi and the killing of Kamsa. The major characters of the epic such as Bhishma, Yudhishthir, Kunti, Gandhari and Draupadi are reinterpreted from an entirely new perspective. The fictional recasting of events and characters has to be carefully examined in the light of Vyasa's epic to explore the significance of deviations. M.N Dutt's translation of the *Mahabharata* in seven volumes has been used as the basic text for all references to study the deviations made in Parva. The transliterated verses from the Sanskrit text of Vyasa, based on *Shriman Mahabharata* by Nag Publishers, Delhi, are given separately wherever necessary. (Problems related to authenticity of the text have been dealt with in Chapter I).

In Bhyrappa's novel, there is a different account of the birth of Karna. He makes Karna the son of Pritha (Kunti) and sage Durvasa. When Kunti was young she was given to her father's friend Kunti Bhoj in adoption. The sage Durvasa paid frequent visits to Kunti Bhoj. Kunti had to attend to his needs and comforts. Her service to the sage brought about an intimacy between the two. This resulted in the birth of Karna. Fearing disgrace Kunti gave away the child to Radha, her mother's friend (67). This account is different from that of Vyasa. In the Adi Parva CXI.7-11 Durvasa is said to have anticipated her future predicament and taught her a mantra to invoke the celestials of her choice to get children: "Through the effulgence of those celestials whom you will invoke by this mantra, offspring will be certainly begotten on you" (Dutt 1:161) Later Kunti is said to have invoked the Sun-God to realize the power of the mantra, "That illuminator of the Universe Tapana (Sun) received her embraces. Thereupon was born a hero known all over the world by the name of Karna" (Ibid).

Later in life, after her marriage, she uses the same mantra to beget sons for Pandu who has lost his procreating powers. The Adi Parva chapter CXXIII 2-5 contains the accounts of the birth of the Pandavas:

> That lady [Kunti] offered adoration to Dharma and repeated in the proper form the Mantra formerly given to her by Durvasa.
>
> The Deity Dharma, being overpowered by the Mantra came on his car resplendent as the Sun to the place where Kunti was seated.

> She was united with Dharma in his Yoga [Spiritual] form and that beautiful lady obtained a son devoted to the good of all creatures. (Dutt 1: 175)

In Vyasa's epic, Pandu entreats Kunti to invoke Dharma (Yama) to beget a son who will lead the Kuru race along with the right path at all times.

> *Āhvayāmasa vai Kuntī garbhārathē dharmam—acyutam //*
>
> Kunti invoked the god Dharma for the sake of conception.

After the birth of the first son who was named Yudhishtir, Pandu wanted a second son who would be endowed with extraordinary strength.

> *Tatas—tathōktva bhartra tu vayum evajuhava sa*
>
> Having been told thus by her husband Kunti invoked the god of the wind.

The second son was named Bhima. Then Pandu thought they must have a warrior-son whose prowess at arms should be unmatched. After a year's penance Kunti prayed to Indra, the chief of Gods for a son of heroic glory.

> *Putram tava prādasyāmi, trisu-lokesu visrutam //* (123.22-23)
>
> Intra told Kunti, "I will give you a son who will be renowned in the three worlds."

In *Parva*, Dharma, Vayu and Indra are not celestial beings but eminent men of the hill tribes called "Devas." Going by the evidence of the practice of polyandry in the Himalayan regions and the story of the Pandavas growing up in these regions in their early age (Adi Parva 126) the novelist has probably chosen to portray the gods as hill tribes called "devas."

The birth of Kauravas is yet another event in the novel that has been recast by Bhyrappa. He dispenses with the myth of Gandhari's hundred sons springing up from a hundred pots. Through the recollections of Gandhari it is reported that Gandhari gave birth to only fourteen sons. She says, "The count of hundred is to the Maharaja's credit. This is his count. But the sons borne by the servant maid with the name Gandhari were only fourteen" (812).

The event has been revisioned by Bhyrappa by demythologizing the account found in Vyasa's epic. In the original epic it is reported that when Kunti gives birth to a son, Yudhishthir, the question of dynastic succession causes concern to Gandhari. Though she has conceived there is inordinate delay in delivering the child. Gandhari certainly, not above jealousy, pounds her abdomen in a fit of anger. The inert fetus has to be cut up and stored as advised by Vyasa. In the Adi Parva CXV 9-20 the account of the birth of the Kauravas is given:

> She bore the burden in her womb for two years without being delivered: she was therefore much afflicted with grief.
>
> [. . .] She struck her womb with violence without the knowledge of Dhritarashtra.
>
> (Vyasa) let one hundred jars filled with ghee to be brought in the proper way; let them be placed at a concealed place and let cool water be sprinkled on this ball of flesh.
>
> O King that ball of flesh in time became gradually one hundred and one separate parts (Dutt 1:165).
>
> *Ghrta-purnam kundasatam ksipram ēva vidhiyatam //*
> *Suguptesu ca dēsēsu raksa caiua vidhīyatam*
> *Sitābhi adbhir asthīlam imām ca pari sincayal* (110.18-19).
>
> (Order a hundred ghee-filled pots to be brought. Keep them in a secret place, protect them and sprinkle cool water on these pieces).

In all these instances Bhyrappa has rejected the ancient myths and views them in terms of human experience. But the novelist says that this was absolutely necessary as his rendering of the epic was to limit it to a strict human possibility. He says:

> In the context of the *Mahabharata* we must understand that myths were intended to explain the incidents which were not acceptable to the changed mores. [. . .] After several centuries they invented myths to explain the Kaninaputra and the Niyoga of Kunti. There is no moral damage to our moral fibre if we frankly accept the mores of our early ancestors as history. (Dandekar 264)

This fictional strategy of demythicising can be viewed as the influence of western scepticism that rejects the superhuman achievements of the ancient Indians. But westerners like Paul Brunton and David Frawley acknowledge the powers of the sages and yogis of India, with awe and amazement. By chanting mantras, ancient sages have been able to work wonders, such as, bringing on the rain, parting and diverting the course of rivers, curing certain illnesses and controlling wild animals. But Bhyrappa's desire to limit the epic to human possibility sets aside the question of biased approach in viewing the ancient myths.

But myths cannot be totally rejected as untrue. In the myth of a foetus being preserved in a hundred pots one finds, indeed, a disconcerting similarity to test-tube babies and cloning of humans. Probably the ancients had their own system of medicines with scientific validity.

M.M. Thakur in *Thus Spake Bhisma* gives almost a similar account of the birth of the Kauravas. Shakuni is said to have impressed upon Dhritarashtra that the "only way to power was through securing a superiority in numbers in the house," Shakuni's project results in the "influx of young Gandharis from distant Gandhara not less than a score of young maids. [. . .] The maidens were all brought into the Palace in strict secrecy and were kept in confinement all through the winter" (49). At the appropriate time the news of the birth of the hundred 'Kauravas' was duly announced. Thakur views the event as a political necessity which later became "the legend of the Hundred Births" (*Ibid*).

Closely linked with the issue of Kunti begetting children through 'Niyoga' is the issue of dynastic succession. The conflict between Pandavas and Kauravas in the novel arises out of Duryodhana's rejection of the right of inheritance of the Pandavas. Duryodhana is unwilling to give the Pandavas their share of the kingdom as they are not, genuinely, the sons of Pandu but only the sons of Kunti. Bhyrappa has depicted the Niyogee fathers of the Pandavas as hill tribes. On account of this lineage Duryodhana denies them the right to ascend the throne.

It may be argued that the hill tribes called 'devas' are the fictional creation of the novelist. Yet, the question of legitimacy of succession remains unsolved, as Kunti has violated the norms of the Niyoga practice. According to the accepted norms of the society, the woman can beget sons at the behest of her husband through ascetic brahmans or her husband's younger brothers. This is not so in the case of Kunti: "yet one thorny issue arises out of this. If there had to be Niyoga why go all the way to the far off Himalayas? Why, instead of getting done through upright Brahmins or husband's brothers, did she have it done through outsiders that too, barbarians from the mountains" (408).

The genuineness of Pandavas' Kuru lineage figures as an issue not only in *Parva* but also in M.T. Vasudevan Nair's *Second Turn.* Duryodhana tells Bhima in a tone of mockery that stories were made up about their births. "In order to hide the identity of the Father, the children were conveniently conceived in the forests. The poor people would believe anything said by the sages. But do you have to repeat that to me, wolf boy?" (33)

Duryodhana's contention in *Parva* is that Kunti has violated the norms of the institution of Niyoga. The conditions laid down for the practice of Niyoga are true to the epic of Vyasa. In the Adi Parva CXX 15-41 there is a reference to the custom of Niyoga. "O greatly fortunate lady like her you too at my command raise offspring by some Brahmana who is superior to me in ascetic merits" (Dutt 1:172).

When Kunti expresses her unwillingness to beget children through anyone other than her husband, Pandu explains to her that it is an accepted custom. "At the time of emergency [failure of offspring], men raise up sons by their accomplished younger brothers" (Dutt 1:171).

In the case of Kunti it is neither Dhritarashtra nor Vidura, who have fathered the Pandavas. The novelist's depiction of gods as hill tribes is in keeping with his intention of dispensing with myths and miracles. He makes an attempt to fit the incidents of the epic into rational structures and inevitably he has to refrain from investing any character with divinity. Whether they are the hill tribes or gods is less important than the corollary of the issue regarding the legitimacy of succession. Viewed from the twentieth century perspective the question acquires great relevance. There are several legal disputes regarding the rights of inheritance of children raised by artificial insemination or by surrogate mothers. The ancients have arrived at amicable solutions to these contentious issues by prescribing codes of conduct of 'Niyoga' as well as succession. Bhyrappa's rejection of myths serves, on the contrary to assert the wisdom of the ancients.

Bhyrappa has recast the episode of Draupadi's disrobing to dispense with divine intervention. The episode of disrobing in the novel is true to Vyasa's epic: "Dushasana was not the one to miss the chance. He came close to me and got hold of my saree's edge. He started to pull it off." (219) This episode occurs in the Dyuta Parva 67.40 of Vyasa's text.

> *Tatō dussāsanō rajan draupadyā vasanam balāt //*
> *Sabhā madhyē samaksi pya vyapakrastum pracakramē //*

> O King! Then Dushasana placing Draupadi in the middle of the assembly began forcefully to pull her robe.

But there are no miracles in *Parva*. Draupadi's honour in the Kuru Sabha is not saved by the miraculous powers of Krishna, but by human intervention. It is Dhritarashtra's fear of Karmic consequences of humiliating a woman to extremity that made him grant her three boons.

In Vyasa's text, Dyuta Parva LXVII 4-48 contains the account of the miracle of protection to Draupadi during Dushasana's disrobing her.

> When Yajnaseni [Draupadi] was crying for protection to Krishna, Vishnu, Hari and Hara the illustrious Dharma remaining unseen covered her with many excellent clothes.
>
> O Lord, in consequence of the protection (extended towards Draupadi) by Dharma, hundreds of cloths of many colour appeared. (Dutt 1:411)

In the novel Krishna is apologetic to Draupadi and Yudhishthir for his absence at the time of the game of dice. It is said that he was in Dwarka:

> I had planned to leave forthwith but at that time Salva was trying to invade Dwarka. He had with him a massive army. But by the time, I

> managed to collect my people, defeat and slay Salva and made sure that no further threat came from his side, it was too late and you had lost everything in the game of dice. (213)

There is sufficient evidence in the Vana Parva Ch XIII to support this view. Krishna tells Yudhishthir, "Having reached Dwarka, O foremost of Kurus, O son of Pandu, I heard all about your misfortune from Yuyudhana" (Dutt 2:24).

Earlier in the beginning of the chapter, he says: "O King of the earth, had I not been then present at Dwarka, O King this misfortune would not have overtaken you" (Dutt 2:23).

Bhyrappa denies divinity to Krishna and portrays him as a member of the Yadava community. Irawati Karve is of the same opinion. She says that the Krishna of the epic is a different character:

> The Krishna shown in the *Mahabharata* has no resemblance at all to the flute-playing lover of milk maids, the divine child or the miracle worker of later tradition. The Krishna in the *Mahabharata* is definitely not a god, as depicted in later literature. He was, however, an extraordinary man, and his great personal ambition was to be called 'Vasudeva.' (167-68)

According to Karve, 'Vasudeva' meant a position approaching divinity if Krishna is not divinity then it follows that the *Gita* is not a sacred text. In *Parva* there is an indirect dismissal of the sacred text, *Gita*, by alluding to Krishna's advice to Arjuna as a kind of indoctrination. In the novel, when Arjuna raised the question of dharma (morality) in fighting one's own kin and his fear of decimating Kshatriya males which could cerate confusion of castes and communities, Krishna tried to bring him round. "Then he took hold of Arjuna and pulled him away to his tent. The whole day, that is, afternoon, evening and night, he talked to Arjuna and indoctrinated him. By yesterday morning it seems he succeeded in restoring Arjuna's mind to its original position" (627).

Myths are inseparable from religious beliefs. Hinduism believes in the theory of rebirth. Bhyrappa is sceptical about such beliefs, and this is expressed through Bhishma's reminiscences:

> All the business of re-birth, is this true? I am sometimes gnawed by doubt. Well, this morning, those two were arguing against such beliefs. They were saying that, whatever cannot be tested by the senses is pure imagination, pure illusion. Maybe those two are right. A eunuch was born to Drupada. But then such children are born to many! Maybe my enemies, intent on destroying me because I have been the backbone of the kuru-kingdom, have mixed up legend and fact so that the eunuch may be triggered to kill me. (615)

Interpretations generally arise out of ideological conceptions. The ideology behind the rejection of myths seems to be rationalism. Myths and miracles are rooted in the beliefs of the community. Lewis Spence in *Introduction to Mythology* says, "The study is assisted by comparative religion, while myths in their turn often explain gods, men and the universe, and customs and organizations of society" (14).

Bhyrappa's fictional strategy of demythologizing the ancient myths is similar to the deconstructive practice of the poststructuralists. The novelist reserves the binary opposition of the sacred and the secular. A secular vision of the epic necessitates the marginalization of the sacred. But Bhyrappa does not totally succeed in destroying the myths. In the process of rejecting the ancient myths, he has created new myths. For instance, examining the cause for the cruelty of Kamsa, Bhyrappa consciously or unconsciously creates a myth about his birth. Kamsa is said to be the son of a Rakshasa. This is narrated through the reflections of Chithra, a companion of Kamsa's mother (332). It is said that Kamsa's mother once lost her way while chasing a deer and reached a secluded part of a forest. There came a Rakshasa, by name Drumila. Drumila is said to be the son of a Rakshasa mother and an Aryan father. Drumila appeared before Kamsa's mother in the garb of her husband, Ugrasena. She mistook him for her husband and out of their union was born Kamsa. This mythical account finds no basis in the text of Vyasa.

In *Parva* Narakasura is portrayed as a highway robber, who is outwitted by Krishna's courage and intelligence:

> Narakasura was a highway robber. Because of him Dwarka had become so insecure that no outsider could arrive there without the sup-

> port of a sufficient number of body-guards. (. . .) If at this time, Krishna's courage endurance and cleverness had not come to our aid, it would have been impossible to hunt him and his band (366).

The creation of new myths testifies to the fact that myths form an integral part of creative process. According to Lewis Spence, "they are mostly explanations of intellectual difficulties, answers to questions as, what is the origin of or reason for this or that phenomenon or custom? How came the world and man to be formed as they are?" (21).

To portray Krishna as a courageous diplomat is intellectually convincing. Tharoor also portrays him as an intellectual. Krishna marrying the women rescued from the tyranny of Narakasura is also given a similar explanation. Though the novelist does refer to the mockery and derision with which this act was viewed, he later offers an insight into the true motive behind it. One of the women remarks, "but for Krishna these women would have drowned in the sea out of despair" (367). Pratibha Ray has also viewed this act of Krishna as an act of social rehabilitation of women.

Bhyrappa has reinterpreted some of the major characters of the epic from a non-traditional perspective. The novelist observes some contradictions in the delineation of major characters such as Bhishma and Yudhishthir. The novelist says, "In the *Mahabharata* the actions of the characters and the opinion on them of their author Vyasa do not always support each other" (Dandekar 258). Contrary to the traditional opinion, Bhyrappa finds Yudhishthir and Bhishma weak characters. According to him Yudhishthir has been idealized in the epic as the epitome of Dharma; but when analyzed in the light of his actions he is found to be a weak character, mean and selfish at times. He says, "Apart from being the Jyestha which was due to the accident of birth, he has no achievements either in war or in management or in solving a crisis" (Dandekar 258).

Bhyrappa accuses him of irresponsibility: "he gambles away the whole of the kingdom earned and developed by his brother's sweat and Krishna's guidance. When it was given back to him by Dhritarashtra's boons to Draupadi, he again gambles it away and makes his wife and brothers go to forest for twelve years and lead a life incognito in the forest for another year" (Dandekar 258).

His lack of self-control and failure to rectify the situation from his own experience hardly justify the reverence with which he has been glorified as 'Dharmaraja.' Such views of Bhyrappa on the character of Yudhishthir are similar to the views expressed by Irawati Karve in *Yuganta*. The question of influence exerted by the earlier work on later writers cannot be ruled out. According to Karve, Dharma could hardly be called a man of action a role demanded by his right to the kingdom.

> Whatever he got was through the valour of others. His beautiful wife, his powerful father-in-law he owed to Arjuna. For protection in both exiles he was indebted to Bhima. Indraprastha and the incomparable Mayasabha were secured by Arjuna and Krishna. The war itself was won through the valour of his brothers and the statesmanship of Krishna. To add to Dharma's humiliation, he had to plead with Arjuna and threaten to renounce the kingdom altogether if Arjuna did not fight. (73)

Karve wonders if he thought it a manly deed to throw to the winds all that others had won for him. Bhyrappa's' inferences are that Vyasa or those who contributed to the growth of the *Mahabharata* idealized Dharmaraja a little too much. He was learned in the traditions and customs of the community and he followed them meticulously. And the myth that he was the offspring of the spiritual element of Yamadharma made the religious-minded people view him with moral awe and their analytical sense was choked (Dandekar 258) The novelist concludes that he is hardly a strong character with integrity.

It can be argued in defence of Yudhishthir that he followed the concept of *Sacivayatta* or the kind of kingship in which the king acts on the advice of the ministers. This is different from *Svayatta* type of kingship in which the king chooses to act on his own. Probably the concept of Sabha, the role of the ministers and the allocation of responsibilities to the King's deputies—all have to be taken into consideration before making a reassessment of Yudhishthir's character. But the fact that besides Bhyrappa, other writers too have expressed similar views cannot be ignored.

Krishna Chaitanya cites an instance of Yudhishthir's unethical behaviour. He says that Yudhishthir found Karna formidable and far superior to Arjuna as a bowman. It is this dread that drives this moralist to the thoroughly immoral intrigue with Salya on the eve of the war to sap Karna's morale. Chaitanya adds: "Yudhishthir's intrigue with Salya, is totally immoral and his rejoicing with all his brothers when Indra obtained Karna's armour and earrings show that he is no angel. [. . .] When self-interest is involved Yudhishthir can be mean like most of us" (135).

T.S. Rukmani in "Moral Dilemmas in the *Mahabharata*" remarks that Dharmaputra was guilty of an immoral act when he uttered loudly within the hearing of Drona "Ashvatthama is dead" and added softly whether the man or the elephant (Matilal 21).

Krishna Chaitanya finds many ambiguities in Yudhishthir's behaviour at the time of disrobing of Draupadi. He says that when Draupadi and Bhima assail Yudhishthir with many arguments during the exile, Yudhishthir accepts their accusations as merited. For he, now, confesses that the had accepted the invitation out of the greedy hope that he would be able to win all the wealth and lands of Duryodhana and appropriate them for himself. In the *Vana Parva* XXXIV, 3, Yudhishthira says, "I was engaged to play at dice with the desire of snatching from Dhritarashtra's son his kingdom with its sovereignty" (Dutt 2:52).

When Keechaka humiliates Draupadi, she bitterly blames the gambler's greed of Yudhishthira which has brought all the suffering upon her. In the *Virata Parva* XVIII, 10, Draupadi says, "You should pass censure on your eldest brother who is solely addicted to the despicable game of dice, through whose act alone I have received this endless woe" (Dutt 2:475). Yet another instance that casts a shadow on Yudhishthir's integrity is cited by Krishna Chaitanya. During the battle he made an offer to Duryodhana that the latter could choose any one of the Pandavas as his adversary and if he won he would be regarded as the victor in the war though he had already lost it. Chaitanya says that this offer has the look of a gambler's ostentatiously reckless challenge:

> All the demands of his integrity could have been met if he had suggested that Duryodhana should fight Bhima with the final victory in the war as the stake. In making the ostentatiously generous offer Yudhishthir does not seem to have given a second's thought to what would have happened if Duryodhana had chosen Nakula or Sahadeva as his adversary. And because of the flawed motives here, he deserves the very sharp upbraiding he gets from Krishna for this indiscretion. (140)

The twentieth century perspective of the character does not give credence to the reverence with which Yudhishthir has been traditionally viewed.

Bhishma is another important character of the epic, found to be flawed. The terrible vow he made and his life-long sacrifice do not in the least exonerate him from his unjust treatment of women. Gandhari in *Parva* makes a taunting remark on Bhishma. While referring to Dhritarashtra's praise of Bhishma's prowess, she says, "of course I have heard that tale of your uncle's habit of interfering in other people's affairs and mismanaging them" (659).

Bhyrappa accuses him of being unfair to Amba, Kunti, Gandhari and Draupadi. Bhishma has ruined the chances of Amba's marriage to Salva by carrying her off as a bride for his half brother. Amba had to immolate herself when she was rejected by both Salva and Bhishma. Amba's grief is referred to in the *Udyoga Parva* of Vyasa's epic.

Amba seeks the help of Rama (Parasurama) to avenge the wrong done to her by Bhishma. She says in the *Udyoga Parva*, CLXXVIII, 38, "The root of this distress of mine is Bhishma of great vows, since by him was I brought under suspicion taking me up by force" (Dutt 3:244). In the same *Parva* CLXXIX, 18, there is a reference to Amba's self-immolation:

> And making a large funeral pyre and having set fire (to it), O monarch, with a mind burning with wrath, even in that flaming fire, the eldest daughter of the King of Kashi, O King, entered the fire on the banks of the river Yamuna. (Dutt 3:258).

In the novel, Bhishma's musings reveal the fact that he felt uncomfortable about Amba's misery: "But I sent back Amba immediately to King Salva. Was I wrong? Did Salva reject her because it would damage his honour and reputation if he now accepted as gift a bride whom he had failed to win through his prowess and valour?" (614)

Bhyrappa's strategy or probing the inner consciousness of the characters through self-introspection, reflections, reminiscence and memories is quite effective in reinterpreting the characters. He makes Bhishma reflect on his own life as one of failures: "He was not so much concerned with the questions of Pandava's defeat or victory, or the survival of mankind itself, in view of the massive armies involved, as the question of whether his whole life has been a total failure in terms of his own ideals" (497).

Bhyrappa holds Bhishma responsible for forcibly arranging the marriages of not only Ambalika and Ambika but also of Kunti, Madri and Gandhari to the Kuru princes who were all either sick or blind or impotent. He was a mute witness to the disrobing of Draupadi. Even his singular aim of propping up the Kuru dynasty was not fulfilled as the kingdom was reduced to smithereens by war, death and disintegration.

The views of Bhyrappa are strengthened by similar opinions of other writers. The women characters that are marginalized in the epic are made to occupy the centre of focus by the contemporary writers. Shashi Deshpande's short story, "The Inner Room" poignantly portrays the agony of Amba who was rejected by both Salva and Bhishma. Amba is depicted as the victim of patriarchal authority. "She was to be disregarded, ignored, her will, her determination had to be set aside as nothing because she was only a woman" (Lal 1:374).

The Bhishma of the epic represents the patriarchal authority. Writers with a feminist perspective denounce his callousness to the sufferings of women particularly to Amba. Bhishma rejected her in order to keep up his vow of celibacy. But, even the genuineness of Bhishma's sacrifice is viewed in sceptical terms by Shashi Deshpande:

> Suddenly Bhishma's "great" act of renunciation appeared to her in its true colours. Of course, she thought, that is how it is. By renouncing his right to the throne and to have children of his own so that his father Shantanu could marry that fisherman's daughter, Satyavati,

> Bhishma let go the shadow and grasped at the substance. He gained power over all of them, his father, his stepmother and their two sons. Power drunk he had become arrogant, uncaring of how he sacrificed others. (Lal 1:373)

Similar views have been expressed by M.M. Thakur, Irawati Karve and M.T. Vasudevan Nair. Thakur's *Thus Spake Bhishma* is a fictionalized autobiography of Bhishma in which he is said to disavow his heroic role, seeing his whole life as a series of acts of his ego. Looking back in remorse Bhishma says, "After Amba was refused by Salva, she undertook a course which finally turned her into the instrument of my eventual fall in Kurukshetra. Considering what my action or lack of it did to her life, what Shikhandi did to me was perfectly just" (30).

Irawati Karve remarks that the injustices done by idealists, patriots, saints and crusaders are far greater than those done by the worst tyrants. "Had Bhishma too become intoxicated by his own public image? (77) Karve suggests that Bhishma was blinded by the very splendour of his renunciation. His concept of dharma reveals only his commitment to the vow of celibacy and lacks far-sighted thinking.

Bhyrappa's portrayal of Yudhishthir and Bhishma is an attempt to reinterpret Vyasa. He finds some discrepancy between the author's intent and execution in relation to the portrayal of these characters. According to the novelist, the actions of the characters hardly merit any attempt to deify them. Bhyrappa's handling of these two idealized characters of the epic goes beyond the traditional parameters of assessment. Bhyrappa's perspective causes a rupture with the tradition, which is what the poststructuralists identify as the core of deconstructive practice. The novelist has attempted a conscious reworking of the past in the light of present socio-political norms. It also reflects the growing awareness of the reader of the epic to develop an unbiased approach in the assessment of the characters by acknowledging their imperfections. The reader of the epic today is not blindly venerating any of the characters who, according to him, are very human. It has often been remarked that the *Ramayana* deals with the ideal whereas the *Mahabharata* is a record of human weaknesses.

Irawati Karve remarks, "In fact the whole *Ramayana* is filled with idealized characters, the ideal brother, the ideal servant, ideal subjects, even ideal villains. It is not that the *Mahabharata* has no extraordinary characters. But, even while depicting the extraordinary person the poet does not let us forget the ordinary in him" (80).

Probably Vyasa also knows that they are 'ordinary' given to weaknesses but draws them as men who had ideals and believed in some standards of dharma as against men who lack any ideal.

There is greater awakening in the society in the recent decades regarding women's rights. Earlier works are examined in the light of rising protests against oppression of women. Bhyrappa seems to evince greater interest in the principles of gender justice and equality. A study of the portrayal of women characters of the epic by the novelist reveals his determination to focus on the marital unhappiness, disappointments and sufferings of major women characters such as Kunthi, Gandhari and Draupadi.

A close examination of the self-reflections and interior monologues of these characters shows that the author has a very humanistic conception of these women characters contrary to traditional image. Bhyrappa's reinterpretation of these characters highlights the marital unhappiness of these women characters in the epic, which has been glossed over so long by attempts to idealize them as archetypes.

Kunti has been idealized as a firm-minded mother who lived to see her sons united in prosperity and adversity. But according to Bhyrappa's novel, Kunti's life as a wife has been sadly ignored in all the earlier versions of the epic. The novelist uses "the stream of consciousness" technique to reassess the character. A study of the flow of thoughts from Kunti's mind, as imagined by Bhyrappa reveals that she does not belong to the tradition of women who worship their husbands. Traditional view of Indian woman lays great emphasis on a faithful and uncomplaining wife. The ideal wife is a 'pativrata' devoted to her husband willing to undergo all kinds of trials and tribulations for the sake of loyalty to her husband. It is a value dearly cherished by ancient Indian women, in following which they achieved great satisfaction. It can be compared to the individual freedom and personal satisfaction experienced by modern women by pursuing a career.

Bhyrappa has shattered the image of a 'pativrata' by portraying Kunti and Gandhari from the humanistic perspective, as emphatically stated by him. In the novel Kunti is depicted as a woman born to endure only sorrow. "What did I get out of life except cruel persecution and stark misery?" (47). Bhyrappa's portrayal of Kunti seems to bear influences of Irawati Karve's study of the character. "Her own father gave her away to a friend. One life-long sorrow was born of this action. "Her adoptive father gave her in marriage to an impotent man and all the rest of her sorrows were a result of this union" (45).

In the novel Kunti has nothing but contempt for her impotent husband. She is repulsed by the very sight of Pandu (52). But Pandu living in a patriarchal society demands an impossible degree of devotion from her by citing Gandhari as a model to be emulated. Little does he realize what was in the mind of Gandhari. In compliance with Pandu's wishes she undergoes "Niyoga" three times. But Kunti is not free from any of the human weaknesses such as ego, jealousy and prejudice. She does not want Madri to have children outnumbering hers. "The fact that Madri bore twins made me jealous of her. I became alert to future possibilities" (97). This aspect of Kunti's character is true to the original. In Vyasa, Pandu requests Kunti to teach the Mantra again to Madri even after she gets twins. But Kunti is firmly against such a proposal. In the *Adi Parva* CXXIV the dialogue between Kunti and Pandu bears out the evidence:

> In private, when the faithful Pritha replied to him thus, "Having given her the Mantra only for once, she has got two sons. I have been deceived by her. I fear she will surpass me in the number of her children. This is the way of all wicked women."

Irawati Karve, commenting on Kunti's fear of Madri establishing her superiority over her says that such rivalry and intrigues among co-wives in Kshatriya households is an important part of Indian history. She says, "To have more sons than the co-wives was also a means of securing, if not the love of a husband, at least the position of the chief queen" (49).

Kunti, in comparison with Madri, appears to be less loyal and devoted to Pandu. On the contrary, Madri is more devoted to Pandu and commits 'Sati' on his death because she thinks that she is indirectly responsible for his death. This act of hers elevates her to the level of a conscientious spouse, if not a worshipper of husband.

In *Parva* Kunti is seen as a prejudiced woman in her relationship with her daughter-in-law. She has nothing but contempt for the Rakshasa wife of Bhima; but she is very fond of Draupadi. Bhima is puzzled by his mother's advice to him to leave Hidimba in the forest and return to the Aryan land. He recalls with anguish that his "mother was unfair and even deceitful in giving her a name" (137). Kunti gives her Aryan name Salakatankati. A change of name will affect one's identity. Bhyrappa seems to depict the relationship from the point of view of racial differences. The Aryan-non Aryan conflict has been emphasized in the novel by Bhyrappa. But recent historical studies point out that Aryan invasion itself is a myth, as Aryans are said to be the indigenous cultural groups in India. David Frawley, Michael Danino and Sujatha Nahar are some of the historians of today who dismiss the theory of Aryan invasion as baseless. David Frawley in *The Myth of the Aryan Invasion of India* says, "We should first note that the Aryan invasion theory was foreign to the history of India, whether north or south; which has no literary or historical record of any such event" (9).

It is an instance of irony that Kunti who cannot be impartial to her daughter-in-law expects Draupadi to treat all her husbands equally. Either Kunti does not want her daughter-in-law to be in any way superior to her having more than one husband or she is advocating the custom of the Deva tribes that a married girl is wife to all her husband's brothers. She becomes the bride of the family. In the novel Draupadi sees it as "an illusion natural for a woman, who had seen the best part of her life without real marital life" (199). Similar idea, expressed by Yajnaseni of Pratibha Ray, has been already discussed in the previous chapter.

Whatever human weaknesses one finds in Kunti, the overall impression that emerges from *Parva* is that Kunti never experienced happiness in her life. Karve remarks that Gandhari and Draupadi, in spite of their suffering, virtually lived as queens; but "Kunti alone among them seems to have been born to endure only sorrow. A dozen years of happiness were too few to compensate for her long life of sorrow and humiliations. Every man in her life contributed to her unhappiness." (43)

Bhyrappa's delineation of the character of Gandhari is similar to that of the character of Kunti. He highlights her suffering on account of her forced marriage to a blind man. From her reminiscences it is evident that the most revered Bhishma was unfair to most women, including Gandhari. To Krishna she expresses her inner anguish, "The marriage was fixed. I thought of running away from home. Even if I had fled, I was sure that Bhishma and his soldiers could have razed our city to ground alleging that my father had deliberately hidden me" (814).

It is reported that Bhishma sent a large contingent of soldiers and cartloads of grains, utensils, ornaments, and jewellery with the message: "these are tokens of friendship. But, if you refuse to offer to my blind son a bride, there is the army, a token of my enmity" (814). Since their military strength could hardly match that of Bhishma in Hastinavati, Gandhari's father was forced to consent to the marriage. Besides, the bride-price he offered was irresistible.

Gandhari out of revulsion and bitterness took a strip of cloth and declared: "if you insist on giving me away in marriage to that blind fellow I shall never set my eyes on him" (814). It is this vow that she kept up till the end. In the eyes of the world, it created an illusion of impossible devotion to her husband. Gandhari recalled that a legend was built around her by heaping praise after praise. Intoxicated by the glory of the legend spun around her, she forgot the real reason behind self-imposed blindness (815) yet, a grouse very painful to her was that her husband had never once asked her to remove the band to enjoy the gift of vision. Such a denial went only to nourish the ego of her husband.

Referring to Gandhari's self-enforced blindness, Krishna Chaitanya remarks: "This is a detail that shares the hyperbole characteristic of epics and one can have doubts about its propriety since a blind husband can hope to see only through the eyes of his life companion" (159).

But according to Vyasa, Gandhari did not want to have any advantage her husband lacked, as referred to, in the *Adi Parva* Chapter CX 14-10. When Bhishma approached Suvala, King of Gandhara for his daughter's hand in marriage to his blind son, Suvala is said to have hesitated at first. But on hearing of the prince's blindness, Gandhari is said to have acted immediately.

> O King, ever devoted to her husband, Gandhari bandaged her own eyes with cloth, gathered into many folds out of her desire that she would not be wanting in respect and love for her husband.
>
> She ever devoted to her husband pleased her superiors by her good conduct and vow—observing as she was, she never referred to other men even in words. (Dutt 1:160).

Gandhari of Vyasa's epic is the archetype of "a pativrata" who stands for an impossible degree of devotion to her husband. The society of the epic period venerated such a woman who underwent a great deal of misery for the sake of loyalty to her husband:

> *Gāndhāntu—atha susrāva dhrtarāstram—acaksusam*
> *Atmanam—ditsutam cāsmai pitrā mātrā ca Bharata*
> *Tatas—sapattam—ādāya krtvā bahu—gunam tadā/*
> *Babandha netre svē rājan pativrata—parayana*
> *Nābhyasuyam patim—aham—ity—evem krtaniscaya* (110. 13-15)

> Then the king, who was willing to give Gandhari in marriage to Dhritarashtra, told Gandhari that Dhritarashtra was blind. Then Gandhari took a silken cloth-piece, folded it and tied it to her eyes in order that she may be on par with her would-be-husband (as far as absence of vision is concerned). She took a firm resolution (and said) on no account will I hate my husband.

Since then the society's attitude has undergone a sea of change. In the twentieth century, suffering of women due to forced marriages invites serious considerations it has been glossed over down the centuries by attempts to idealize women as archetypes.

Irawati Karve's historical study of the character also refers to Gandhari as a wronged woman. Her marriage to Dhritarashtra was a trick played on her. She was brought from Gandhara to Hastinavati to marry Dhritarashtra without being told of his blindness. Her companion told her, "you are betrayed, poor darling. We are betrayed, the prince you are going to marry is blind from birth. For a moment Gandhari did not comprehend her friend's words. The next moment, she fell to the floor unconscious" (32).

M.T. Vasudevan Nair also gives such a twist to the incident. The novel is a first person narrative from Bhima's point of view. Bhima refers to the marriage of Gandhari and says, "Aunt knew only when the wedding rites were on that her bridegroom the Prince Dhritarashtra was blind" (28).

According to Karve, towards the end, Dhritarashtra seeks forgiveness from Gandhari for the dishonest trick played on her. After the war Dhritarashtra having lost all his sons decides to leave for the forest and tells Dharma about his decision. Vidura supports him. Kunthi decides to join them. "Nobody asked Gandhari for her opinion. Everyone assumed that her husband's wish was hers. In the forest Dhritarashtra and Gandhari give vent to their frustration, looking back at their past in regret. Dhritarashtra admits to Gandhari, 'You were deceived. Without being told of my blindness you were married to me. We did you a thousand wrongs Gandhari. But you have paid them back; can't you ever forgive and forget?'" (37) The twentieth century perspective highlights the need for a psychological understanding of the characters particularly the women.

Bhyrappa's delineation of Draupadi's character is also from the point of view of her marital life. It is a myth that she was able to love all her husbands equally. To be the common wife of all the five brothers was a challenge to her physically and mentally. It puzzled Draupadi herself how her gentle self got the strength to manage the aggression of five husbands. She was particularly attached to Bhima whom she found to be her "only refuge." He was the only one who could understand her half-expressed wishes, thoughts and interruptions. "It was Bhima who worked himself to death to save her modesty, after the game of dice when Dushasana stripped her of her single cloth, when Jayadratha wanted to marry her off in the forest and when Kichaka aspired for her" (135). The question of loving all her husbands equally and other related charges and accusations arise only in patriarchal society. Draupadi is portrayed as a woman denied gender justice. Bhima could not love all his wives equally. Arjuna could not treat all his wives alike.

In Draupadi's reminiscences, her marital life is reportedly one of suffering: "Conception after conception, children, post natal period and again marital life. This eighteen year old, bubbling with life was transformed into an exhausted twenty four year old, a worn out cow" (199). She recalled that it was a suicidal onslaught on her body to preserve the unity of Pandava brothers.

It is noteworthy that Draupadi's revelations cast Yudhishthir in a poor light. The cause, for the fall of Pandavas was Yudhishthir's weakness for the game of dice and the unethical act of using his wife as a stake in gambling. Dharmaraja, supposed to be the embodiment of Dharma, practically failed to uphold the values of Dharma. In this context it is worth recalling the great Tamil Poet Bharathi's words in *Panchali Sapatam* 19-126.

> *Tharuman*
> *Ennang Kalangich chila sol uraippaan*
> *Manru punaindadhu kettumichi choodhin*
> *Vaarthai yaik kettuming genran manaththe*
> *Chenru varuththam Ulaikindra thiaiya*
> *Chindaiyil aiyyam vilaikiurathaiya* (435)

> Dharma, mentally agitated, said, "When I heard that the sabha is arranged for the game of dice, my mind is troubled with doubts and fears. This news gives me great sorrow."

According to Bharathi, Yudhishthir was reluctant to accept the invitation to play dice as evident in his reply to Vidura who met him with the message from Duryodhana. In Bhyrappa's novel there is no such hesitation on the part of Yudhishthir. Draupadi is sore over Dharmaraja's failure to understand her, "this Dharmaraja who started his day with discussion with Vedic experts didn't know this vedic dictum" fretted Draupadi (231).

In Bharathi's *Panchali Sapatam* 66-281 Bhima burst out that the hands of the one who staked Draupadi in the game of dice should be burnt:

> *Ithu poruppathillai Thambi*
> *Erithazhal Kondu vaa*
> *Kathirai Vaithizahandhan—annan*
> *Kaiyai erithiduvom* (485)

> We cannot put up with this. Bring the burning coals. Let us set ablaze the hands of our elder brother, who staked and lost the light of our lives.

Dharma is the main source of her miseries, according to Draupadi, "This Dharma who had been the main source of all my miseries ceased to talk to me face to face" (231). Even the anomalous situation of her polyandrous marriage would have been averted if Dharma had not coveted her. Referring to the context, Draupadi says, "he did not stop stealing looks at me all the while" (188). All the brothers were falling foul of each other because of their infatuation with Draupadi. According to Bhyrappa, Kunti even threatened to return Draupadi to her father to prevent conflict among brothers. Her sole aim in life was to keep the Pandavas united in order to get the throne.

In *Adi Parva* 190.2 of Vyasa's epic, Kunti is said to have told her sons to share equally what they had won without seeing what they had won:

> *Kutīgatā sā tuanauksya putrav*
> *Prōvāca bhunktēti sametya sarve /*
> *Pascācca Kuntī prasamīksya krsnām*
> *Kastam mayā bhāstitam Ityuvāca //*

> Without looking at her sons Kunti told them, "share it equally and eat it (enjoy it)." Afterwards Kunti saw Krsna (Draupadi) and said, "I have committed a blunder in telling (my sons) to share (their earning) equally and eat it (enjoy it)"

Bhyrappa deviates from the epic and shows Pandavas' infatuation with Draupadi leading to the strange case of her polyandry. He has marginalized the role of Kunti in effecting such a marriage. There is no reference in the novel to Kunti's injunction to share equally what they have won, through Draupadi is suspicious of Kunti's motives. Nor does Bhyrappa refer to Drupad reacting against it. Drupad expresses his shock at the proposal in Vyasa's text. In *Adi Parva* CXCVII 27-28 Draupadi tells Yudhishthir,

> O descendant of Kuru, it is ordained that a husband can have many wives, but we have never heard that a wife can have many husbands.
>
> O son of Kunti pure as you are and acquainted with the rules of morality, you should not commit an act that is sinful and opposed both to the Vedas and usage. Why has your understanding come to be so? (Dutt 1:268)

Krishna Chaitanya also says that Drupad was shocked when he heard that Draupadi was to be the wife of five men and rejected the proposal as unheard of and immoral (146). Drupad's objection is referred to in M.M. Thakur's *Thus Spake Bhisma* also: "Drupad admitted to me later that he was not prepared at all, for such an eventuality" (101) referring to his daughter's predicament of having to marry the Pandava brothers. Draupadi's polyandrous marriage has drawn the attention of several critics.

A.N. Jani in "Moral Dilemmas in the *Mahabharata*" says that the custom of polyandry was prevalent in ancient times not only in India but in other countries too such as North and South America, Africa, New Zealand, Tibet and Sri Lanka. In the Himalayan region, it was an accepted custom:

> It prevails even today among the Todas of the Nilgiri Hills. Among the Nairs of Kerala and in the northern part of Sikkim it is prevalent even today. This custom seems to have originated out of social necessity in those regions where the number of females was less than that of males. In some places it came into existence with a view to keeping the family wealth, in one place. Elsewhere it originated from the problem of protection of a woman whose husband was away from home for a very long time. Thus the custom originated out of the social and economic needs of the peoples concerned. (Matilal 72)

Though historical evidence of existence of the polyandry is cited by many, Bhyrappa reduces the entire situation to an act of human weakness. The novelist has also wrapped up the story of the epic with post-Kurukshetra gloom permeating the entire novel. Sanjaya functioning like Greek chorus reports to Dhritarashtra the miserable scenes of the battlefield:

> How can I say? Who can count how many thousands of men died in the last ten days of the fighting, how many got wounded with their limbs torn and blood flowing? When an event took place in one place, it is no longer a site of action the next day. Why? The dead men, the dead horses, the dead elephants rot and exude terrible stench. (661)

Bhyrappa evokes a poignant picture of the dead and the dying:

> Countless horses yoked to the chariot and used by the cavalry, lay, writhing in death agony, their legs broken or crushed. As the horses put out of action in the battle cannot be driven back, they had to remain there. The only use for them was to carve out their meat. As the dead animals piled up and their blood flowed into rivers, the other horses ran helter-skelter. The death-cries of fallen soldiers reached one's ears even in that battle confusion and noise. (722)

The vivid description of bloodshed and horror, death and destruction creates a sense of colossal waste everywhere:

> Blood flowing and solidified, flies buzzing, fallen bits of warrior equipment, necklaces torn from necks, ear-rings torn from their ears, heads hanging from mutilated trunks and all sorts of head gear rolled away from the heads of the dead and the lost. [. . .] How much can one man's memory carry off that awesome sight? One thing was certain. Everything there was broken, destroyed, damaged, dying, dead and rotting. And the packs of wild animals feasting on flesh and blood with total abandon. (727)

V.S. Sukthankar in *On the Meaning of the "Mahabharata"* examined the story on the ethical plane and commented on the cosmic dimensions of the epic:

> What gives the trivial tale of petty jealousy, intrigue and strife [. . .] real depth and significance is the projection of the story on to a cosmic background, by its own interpretation of the Bharata war as a mere incident in the ever-recurring struggle between the Devas and the Asuras; in other words, as a mere phase in cosmic evolution. [. .] This war—or to give it a more general name conflict—is an eternal recurrence, a phenomenon assuming in the space-time continuum

> the most diverse forms and aspects. The *Mahabharata* thus becomes the type or the *archetype* of all wars or conflicts of the past, the present or the future. (63)

The futility and colossal waste of human energy and resources causing an oppressive gloom after the end of the war are effectively brought out by Bhyrappa. T.S. Eliot in *The Wasteland* also, through the vision of Tiresias, refers to this universal fact that all wars are one and the same in the sense, the ultimate result of a sense of vacuum and nothingness is common to all wars.

The novel *Parva* is also remarkable for the environmental concerns expressed in the novel. The pollution created by the carcasses and foul stench of the battlefield pose the greatest threat to environment. Bhyrappa refers to the acute water scarcity suffered by the soldiers in the battlefield. Duryodhana had to face the problem of feeding and housing his supporters. All classes of workers demanded their wages whether there was work or not. War was draining out the economic resources of the country. Even the saints and the sages had to surrender the property of the hermitage to the King, as it was believed that all the land in the country belonged to the king. General resentment of men for compulsory enlisting in the army, the fear and panic of soldiers, their apprehension and sense of insecurity are all vividly portrayed in the novel.

Bhyrappa's novel can be considered as a sub-text of Vyasa's *Mahabharata*. The main text, the original epic provides the core and the sub-text deals with the selection of materials from the core. Vyasa's text is an objective report of events; it just narrates what happened, without offering a commentary or interpretation. Creative writers have exploited this absence of interpretation in Vyasa and have chosen to draw their own conclusions and interpretation. The reader of the epic is inspired to rewrite, to recreate, the epic to suit the changes in the socio-political conditions of his times. It is evident in *Parva* that the novelist has used the text to express his ideology, to lend a rational credibility and humanistic approach to ancient myths. One cannot miss the contemporary relevance of the novel.

Intertextuality seems to be more complex, observes Sethuraman in "Resonance and Intertextuality." The term signifies the interdependence of any one literary text on or interrelationship with all those that have gone before it. According to Sethuraman, a text is just a mosaic of quotations. "Texts absorb and transform one another. Meanings from one kind of discourse are overlaid with meaning from another kind of discourse; and the creative artist is rather a synthesizer, someone who draws together and orchestrates linguistic raw materials, than an inspired maker" (154).

Bhyrappa has successfully synthesized the core of the main text, and produced a different text that reinforces the contemporary relevance of the epic, the *Mahabharata*. He has adopted an effective combination of narrative techniques such as reflections, reminiscences and interior monologues. Such techniques, absent in the text of Vyasa, contribute to fresh insights into the original.

In the process of reinterpreting the epic from a twentieth century perspective, Bhyrappa has challenged the archetypal figures in Vyasa's epic. Paradoxically the challenge has invested the ancient classic with a value reasserted time and again. Referring to the rewritings of literary classics, John McLeod observes: "rewriting will always invest value in the source-text as a point of reference, no matter how much it is challenged as a consequence" (169) Bhyrappa's *Parva* takes Vyasa's *Mahabharata* as a point of inspiration as well as departure but the interrogation of the source text ultimately serves to enrich the value of the epic.

Chapter V

Conclusion: Tradition and Contemporary Relevance

At the threshold of the twenty-first century, India seems to face great challenges. Failure of democracy, political uncertainty, cultural invasion by the West, communal violence and the hegemony of religious fundamentalism of all types are the harsh realities confronting India. India today no longer represents the lofty culture of her glorious past. One way of comprehending the present and coming to terms with it is by visualizing what India means to herself. In order to do this, one must necessarily examine how the two great epics have affected the Indian mind. Creative artists explore the past through a study of the ancient works and see their relevance to the present. The novels chosen for study help us to see the direction in which our culture will progress.

An objective record of the past without prejudices and distortions by the historians is not available. Two hundred years of British rule has left a strong legacy. The colonized mind tends to devalue Indian culture and tradition. The sacred aspects of Indian culture are derided as profane and impracticable. On the contrary, some western thinkers and historians have admitted a biased approach to the assessment of Indian culture and history. David Frawley in *Gods, Sages and Kings* states that the Western historians have presented a distorted account of India:

> So far we have interpreted the culture and history of India according to our own social, intellectual and religious preconceptions and have thereby created a distortion of it. By distorting it, we have distorted our own history and that of the world as a whole which is all interrelated. In fact our treatment of the ancient spiritual teachings of India

> is just the most evident way in which we have misinterpreted the ancient world and its spiritual background. We interpret ancient scriptures and mystical texts by modern social and psychological ideas and quite naturally find them to be chaotic or primitive. By the spiritual standards of the ancients, our modern intellectual and material culture may be found lacking as well. (24)

A true picture of India emerges in the unprejudiced assessment of ancient India. Ancient India is acknowledged by many western scholars as the source of all knowledge and wisdom. Michael Danino and Sujata Nahar in *The Invasion that Never was* say that "the Indian civilization has lasted through the ages because it knows to hold on to its essential strength and spirit and how to evolve with it. [. . .] Today's challenges will not be overcome by abandoning this strength and spirit" (145). They endorse Will Durrant's assertion of the greatness of India that "India was the motherland of our race and Sanskrit the mother of Europe's languages. India was the mother of our philosophy, of much of our mathematics, of the ideals embedded in Christianity [. . .] of self-government and democracy. In many ways, modern India is the mother of us all" (141). Such observations by the westerners falsify the colonial interpretation of western culture as the pinnacle of human civilization. It is worth-noting that in the twentieth century, many European writers came up with the opinion that after the unprecedented barbarism of the two world wars, it is foolish to look upto the West as the centre of enlightenment.

The Indian novelists have time and again turned to the two great Indian epics to explore the values of the past to facilitate an understanding of the present. As Chinua Achebe has put it in his "The Novelist as Teacher," the novelist has to function as an educator of the community. The constant effort at recreating and retelling the *Mahabharata* bears evidence to the writer's quest for discovering the presentness of the past. Romila Thapar in *Interpreting Early India* argues the importance of understanding and positioning various well-established perspectives on the Indian past in order to arrive at an informed understanding of the contemporary situations. In "Society and Historical consciousness, The Itihasa Purana Tradition," she says, "Each version of the past which has been deliberately transmitted has a significance for the present and this accounts for its legitimacy and its continuity. The record may be one in which historical consciousness is embedded: myth, epic and genealogy" (138).

Thapar's view of the epic as a record of the embedded historical consciousness bears similarly to the view of Page du Bois, recorded much earlier. "History, man's reading of the past, is part of poetry, especially in the epic and that its use in poetry is part of the attempt to control the present and shape the future of human community" (2). T.S. Eliot in "Tradition and Individual Talent" says that it is the historical consciousness that makes the writer most acutely conscious of his place in time, of his own contemporaneity (14). It is for this reason that the two great Indian epics are considered the classics of world literature. A classic according to *Random House Dictionary of the English Language* refers to any literary work that is of first or highest rank and honoured as definitive in its field. Frank Kermode in *The Classic* recognizes antiquity as an essential feature of a class (5). He says,

> The doctrine of a classic as model or criterion entails in some form the assumption that the ancient can be more or less immediately relevant and available in a sense contemporaneous with modern or any way that its nature is such that it can by strategies of accommodation be made so. [. . .] This modern is a renewal of the ancient. Still renewing the past changes our sense of it. The greatest of the renovation, the one we call the Renaissance did that too; it is also the best illustration of the truth that efforts to see the models clearly make them seem further off in time. (167)

It is indeed the aspect of perpetual contemporaneity that makes the work a classic. Kermode refers to Arnold's criterion, that it is required of the classic that it should enable us to think of its age and our own together" (19). Further he says, "Eliot also accepted this criterion of the contemporaneity of the classic and the concomitant doctrine that history is under all the appearance of change a unity; that the modern is not absolutely new, but a renovation of a classic which the action of time has obscured and which now reappears in a new relationship with the modern. [. . .] Tradition is the word for continuum, tradition is the historical agent of renovation" (21).

The two great Indian epics fulfill all the requirements of a classic antiquity, perpetual contemporaneity and immediate relevance. Romila Thapar seems to see a happy combination of the eternal and the temporal in the epic idiom of India when she says in *Exile and Kingdom*, "The idiom therefore is of the new times with nostalgia for the old" (1).

The epic displays events and situations that can be compared to the contemporary context. George Lukacs in "The Epic and the Novel" in his *The Theory of the Novel* says that the content of the epic has a universal quality about it. "World destiny [. . .] is what actually gives the events of the epic their content; the epic hero, as a bearer of his destiny connects him by indissoluble threads to the community whose fate is crystallized in his own" (67). Several writers who have fictionalized the epic have tried to form a link between the past and the present. As Lukacs says, "The novel is the epic of the age in which the extensive totality of life is no longer directly given, in which the immanence of meaning in life has become a problem yet which still thinks in terms of totality" (56).

The study of the re-rendering of the *Mahabharata* takes the reader into the interdisciplinary terrain where mythology, religion, philosophy and history meet. It is difficult to view the epic totally either as myth or as history. The myth is a kind of poetic reincarnation of history. The report of the Associate Press in *The Hindu Business Line* refers to some historical basis for the myth of "Jason and the Golden Fleece," in "Timeless Classic of Jason Revisited."

> Since ancient times Jason's quest for the Golden fleece was told as purely a mythical epic. [. . .] Excavations may uncover some truth behind the tale. Archaeologists digging in the foothills of Mount Pelican in central Greece have uncovered a Mycenaean city and palace complex, which they believe may have provided the inspiration for one of the most enduring Greek fable, the adventures of Jason and his Argonauts. The excavation in Dimini about 170 km northwest of Athens shows evidence it was a major trading centre for the Aegean and Black Sea region. The gold used for jewellery for example was likely brought to Greece by seafaring traders. [. . .] "Maybe

> this myth of the Argonaut campaign is a memory of these quests to bring back raw materials, to bring back metals" said Adrimi.

Vasso Adrimi seems to have directed the excavation since it started in 1978. Similarly excavations carried out in the sites associated with the epic *Mahabharata* indicate some historical basis for the story of the epic. N.V.R. Krishnamacharya in his *The Mahabharata* refers to the views of the archaeologist B.B. Lal on the historicity of the *Mahabharata.* According to B.B. Lal, excavations carried out in all sites associated with the *Mahabharata* such as Hastinapura (Meerut District, UP), Barnawa (Varnavata, UP), Birata (Viratanagar, Jaipur), Indraprasta (Delhi) and Kurukshetra (Haryana) give circumstantial evidence suggesting that in all likelihood there was a basis for the story which as time passed, got inflated out of all proportions to the original (466). Krishnamacharya discusses the importance of myth in the light of the views of Nihar Ranjan Ray. According to Ray, myth is neither fictional nor illusory; a myth is neither a legend nor a mere fable. In actuality it is a true story of the life of any society, the essence extracted out of the very process of human life of a given time and space. A myth is an extremely complex cultural reality, the foremost function of which is to reveal the exemplary models of all significant human activities in a given society from birth to death. Indeed myths are the most proud and meaningful possession of early pre-industrial revolution societies, since the deep-rooted traditions provide living entities in the sense that they supply models of human behaviour and by doing so give meaning and value to the flowing current of life in a given social situation. A myth is a socio-psychological phenomenon and hence a reality which historians can hardly afford to ignore (477).

Since the epic provides models of human behaviour, writers frequently turn to the epic to explicate conditions of the present. Several layers of meaning are unfolded to the discerning eye. Romila Thapar in *Exile and the Kingdom: Some Thoughts on the Ramayana* says, "It is now recognized that epic literature is composed of many layers of consciousness some of which layers receded into the subconscious. It is this, which allows versatility in the interpretation of epic material. Historians working on the Indian epics have largely concentrated on the virtually impossible task of dating the epics, trying to authenticate the events or using the fragments as source material on a variety of subjects" (1).

As several layers of cultural experience are embedded in the epic, it is difficult to separate the historical and fictional elements from the content of the epic, N.K. Sidhanta in *The Heroic Age of India* observes that heroic poetry contains a certain amount of fact and fiction fused together:

> The question of myth making leads us on to that of creative fiction in the heroic poem. Following Aristotle we may say that poetry is never the same as history, that it is a more philosophical and a higher thing than history; for poetry tends to express the universal, history the particular. In other words the imagination of the poet is never content merely to record facts; it must seek to idealize them to make them as they ought to be rather than as they are. This implies a certain amount of fiction in poetry even in poems based on fact, in poetical accounts of events. [. . .] Heroic poems dealing as they often do with the more distant and less definitely known past are bound to contain a larger amount of fiction. (107)

It is this fusion of fact and fiction that gives infinite scope of interpretation. Writers have identified aspects of perpetual contemporaneity in the epic and recast them in the fictional mode. The process of fictionalizing these works chosen for study involves mythologizing and demythologizing, historicizing the myth and mythologizing history. Shashi Tharoor mythologizes some of the events of history and historicizes some of the events of the epic in *The Great Indian Novel* and brings out the contemporary relevance of the epic. He identifies the craving for political power as the common motif for the ruin of both the ancient Hastinapura and the modern India. The adoption of the framework of the epic to his novel enables him to make a political satire of the history of modern India. Pratibha Ray highlights the predicament of the women and the oppressed group through the character of Draupadi of the epic. Bhyrappa draws the attention of the reader to certain issues of socio-cultural importance that are relevant to the 20th century. He highlights the suffering of the women characters of the epic and accuses the author of having idealized the characters of Bhishma and Yudhishthir a little too much. He holds these two men characters as having been responsible for the misery of women characters. The novelist says that his endeavour to reduce the whole of the *Mahabharata* to strict human possibility led to the destruction of myths in the novel.

Bhyrappa's deliberate attempt at destroying the myths requires a careful examination. As pointed out in the Introduction myths form a part of the racial memory. They are carried forward from generation to generation as an essential part of a cultural ensemble. In his zeal to destroy myths and miracles from the purview of his novel he has created new myths, consciously or unconsciously in place of ancient myths. This is a sure proof of the fact that myths form an integral part of the creative process in any literary creation. In the delineation of the character of Krishna he has dispensed with the aspect of divinity and portrays him as merely the king of the Yadavas; but while examining the cause for the wickedness of Kamsa, the author ends up by creating a mythical account of his birth. Yet another instance is the myth of Narakasura as a highway robber.

The myth of begetting children through chanting of mantras is dismissed by Bhyrappa. Karna is portrayed as the son of Kunti and Durvasa. The Pandavas are shown as Kunti's sons fathered by eminent men of the hill tribes called 'devas' through the practice of 'Niyoga.' The myth is viewed in terms of human experience. The tendency of an Indian writer to question the ancient Indian myths seems to be an expression of western scepticism. The unmistakable influence of the colonial legacy reveals itself in the rejection of esoteric practices prevalent in ancient India.

Some westerners record the greatness of ancient Indian civilization with awe and amazement. David Frawley in *Gods, Sages and Kings* acknowledges the special occult knowledge possessed by Vedic Aryans.

> While they knew a great ideal of the secret forces of nature, their knowledge worked through the mind rather than through technology. Meditation or mantra was the main force used. It allowed them to travel great distances, to bring on the rain and to part the rivers for

> people to cross. They kept their knowledge secret, veiled in a mystery region and allowed majority of people to follow a simpler outer life in harmony with nature. (38)

Myths are inseparable from the religious faith of the community. Christianity too is based on the miraculous which is seldom questioned. Belief in the Immaculate Conception is one such example. Christ walked on water and raised Lazarus from the dead. If these are accepted as facts, then there is no reason to reject the myth of begetting children by chanting of mantras. Paul Brunton in *A Search in Secret India* asserts that the West has much to learn from the Indian sages of the past and from the few who live today. His encounter with the Yogis who are adept at performing miraculous feats is recorded in his book. He says, "The secret India's spiritual life still exists despite the storms of political agitation which now hide it and I have tried to give authentic record of more than one adept who has attained strength and serenity for which we lesser mortals wistfully yearn" (7). He refers to the incredible powers possessed by Yogis such as Hazrat Babajan the woman Faqueer, Upasani Maharaj, Shri Shankara, Maharishi Ramana, Badreenath Sathu, Sahabji Maharaj, Yogi Ramiah. Paul Brunton concludes with a wish to be engulfed in the positive aura of these sages and yogis. Brunton's affirmation that those who close their minds to the entrance of all Eastern ideas, close them also to fine thoughts, deep truths worthwhile psychological knowledge, is the richest testimony to the ancient wisdom of India.

Bhyrappa's attempt to eliminate myths from his work is probably necessitated by his secular vision of the epic. Joseph Campbell in *The Hero with a Thousand Faces* refers to such inevitability as civilization advances:

> In the later stages of many mythologies the key images hide like needles in great haystacks of secondary anecdote and rationalization; for when a civilization has passed from a mythological to a secular point of view, the olden images are no longer left or quite approved. In Hellenistic Greece and in Imperial Rome, the ancient gods were reduced to mere civil patrons, household pets and literary favourites. The uncomprehended inherited themes, such as that of the Minotaur—the dark and terrible night aspect of an old Egypto-Cretan rep-

> resentation of the incarnate Sun-god and divine-king were rationalized and reinterpreted to suit contemporary ends. (248)

The process of demythologizing ancient myths in *Parva* cannot be considered to be the outcome of a change of civilization but a rationalistic view of the individual writer. Indian tradition has never put Reason and Faith in confrontation, a confrontation which elsewhere has repeatedly resulted in the rejection of Faith on the grounds of Reason or of Reason on the grounds of Faith. India has postulated a reality that is supra-rational, not irrational. Her intellectual and spiritual horizons are so wide that there is no concept of heresy and the definition of religion includes atheism. Diversity, not uniformity, is accepted as the norm and India has implicitly accepted racial, religious, cultural, ethnic or other differences as normal.

India's comprehensive view of the universe has ruled out a homocentric vision which has prevailed in the West. India has never accepted that the rest of creation was put there for man's benefit. At different levels and in different ways, it was put across that the entire universe, animate and inanimate, is one and imbued with divinity; that mere matter and material forms are mutable, inconstant and illusory (Maya). Even in such matters as the disciplining of the body, India's yoga system not only sets a different method but also a different objective for the exercise.

India's acceptance of diversity, often called its tolerance, is a better model for future world society, than the existing models of uniformity and intolerance, whether of race, religion, political ideology or other factors. What is more, not only does a philosophy of homogeneity and conformity not correspond to, actually, but it limits our capacity for comprehension. Bhyrappa claims to be realistic in his approach by breaking through some of the myths in the *Mahabharata*. He says, "In the context of the *Mahabharata* we must understand that myths were invented to explain the incidents which were not acceptable to the changed mores. [. . .] There is no damage to our moral fibre if we frankly accept the mores of our early ancestors as history" (Dandekar 264). Perhaps his desire to reduce the epic to strict human possibility is fulfilled by fitting the mythical episodes of the epic into rational structures. But Joseph Campbell says that "Whenever the poetic myth is interpreted as biography, history or science, it is killed" (249). The essential spirit of the Indian tradition has not been taken into consideration by Bhyrappa as he rejects Faith in favour of Reason.

The function of myth in any age is to deal with the human predicament. This involves examining socio-cultural issues and conflicts and setting up a paradigm for analysis, and resolution. This has happened in Vyasa's epic. When modern writers go back to the epic they do it for the same purpose, thus legitimizing the epic. Some of the problems confronted by humanity in the present are similar to the problems that existed in the past. Problems of women and the oppressed group, war of succession and rights of inheritance are some of the socio-cultural issues of the present which have not been without precedents in the past.

Pratibha Ray sees in the story of Draupadi the need to champion the cause of the oppressed. In an interview given to Sue Dickman in the *Book Review* Ray says that she has challenged the whole world through Draupadi:

> My Draupadi is not the Draupadi of the *Mahabharata.* I have written that novel in the background of that story. [. . .] I have dealt with all the contemporary social problems, social issues. I have challenged the whole world through Draupadi about the contemporary situation in politics, in social life, everything. But people say that I have portrayed the misery and agony of women. It is not that; critics are very unfair. Unfair, meaning I think they have not understood clearly if it is written by a woman, then it is only about women's suffering. I have written that novel, so I know. My message is no war, no violence, world peace, national integration and international understanding. (33)

Pratibha Ray interprets the story of Draupadi on a social plane and finds it a tale of caution to the world that oppression and tyranny, be it in the past or present, will end in disastrous consequences. As claimed by the novelist in the interview quoted above, the contemporary social situation of the oppressed group is in no way different from that of Draupadi of the epic. The epic mirrors human condition time and again and hence the writers draw inspiration from the epics to come to terms with the present. The social status of a woman depends on her education, marriage and children. The epic *Mahabharata* has dealt with issues related to women's problems such as polygamy, polyandry and 'Niyoga.' Inevitably myths have been used to explicate some of these social conditions. Romila Thapar says that some myths legitimize a social condition. In *Interpreting Early India*, she examines the function of myths:

> The epic as the literature of one age looking back nostalgically on another can become a literature of legitimation. [. . .] That legitimacy and validation are essential to the epic is clear from the central event of the narrative, namely the legitimacy of succession, involving elder and younger sons and the problems of disqualification. [. . .] Legitimacy also relates to using the past to explain the present. Perhaps the most dramatic example of this to the series of explanations is in favour of accepting the strangeness of Draupadi marrying five brothers, a fraternal polyandry not being a commonly practiced form of marriage. Among the explanations, is predictably a reference to an earlier birth of Draupadi, (150)

In *Parva* Duryodhana raises the question of the genuineness of the kuru lineage of the Pandavas as they were begotten by Kunti through the practice of 'Niyoga.' The war of succession in the epic can be compared to a plethora of legal disputes over rights of inheritance by children raised by scientific innovations such as artificial insemination or hiring of surrogate mothers. What the ancients foresaw as a serious problem and arrived at a practical solution by introducing a system called Niyogi framed according to the acceptance norms of that age surfaces in the present. This problem has assumed serious social and psychological dimensions today.

The West now approves of various means of begetting children, more or less similar to the custom of Niyoga, recognized by the ancient Indians to be the only alternative arrangement that works. Thus the precedents in the past seem to offer valuable guidance to the present. Several social and cultural changes in the western society can be construed as attempts to arrive at amicable solutions to questions of irreconcilable issues. India has recognized all these afflictions of humanity even in ancient times.

In the postcolonial era, the 'modern intellectual' has a tendency to dismiss the ancient wisdom in the same way that the Europeans did. The precedents set up by the wisdom of the ancient India have not always been well-projected by the historians and western-educated intellectuals in India. The issue of bias cannot be ruled out in the writing of history. Warren Fusfeld in "Indifference to Religious Sources for Political History" in *Bias in Indian Historiography* says: "History is all that has happened, not what is written by historians. Rather, historians record some selection and sometimes an interpretation of a part of what has happened. It is the process of selection which is the ultimate cause of bias and it cannot be avoided" (Devahuti 30). Fusfeld finds "some historians attempting to write about Indians in British India but have chosen for study those groups who were most outspoken, either in opposition to the British or with respect to the condition of Indian society with an eye to reforming it, so as to make it more congruous with the sense of what was 'modern' and therefore more correct" (31). Fusfeld says that the term 'modern' was synonymous with Western and hence "the study of such reformers also tends to present us with a view from a Western or British perspective" (31).

The treatment of ancient myths in *Parva* might make the reader suspect bias in the approach of Bhyrappa. But his desire to keep to the current trends in the society as revealed in his secular vision is quite evident in the novel.

Tharoor's *The Great Indian Novel* can be viewed in a way as a reaction against colonial interpretation of Indian history and culture as mentioned earlier. Bill Ashcroft in 'Allegory' in *Post Colonial Transformation* finds postcolonial aspects of history evident in Tharoor's novel:

> By interpolating the *Mahabharata*'s sense of the timeless and recurrence of historical events, the power of the imperial, empirical history of India is undetermined in a kind of allegorical one-up man ship. [. . .] The embracing syncreticity of the process by which the positive transparency of the *Mahabharata* adds a layer of narrative to those already in existence is one which provides rich possibilities for the project of a post-colonial history. The writer's India is therefore one which becomes endlessly redefinable. (108)

The evolutionary nature of history itself as a process of selection and interpretation is reaffirmed by Tharoor:

> History, Ganapathi—Indeed the world, the universe and all human life and so too, every institution under which we live is in a constant state of evolution. The world and everything in its being created and recreated even as I speak, each hour, each day, each week going through the unending process of birth and rebirth which has made us all. India has been born and reborn scores of times and it will be re-born again. India is for ever; and India is for ever being made. (245)

All these attempts at reacting against the Eurocentric interpretation of Indian history are a powerful effective strategy of offering cultural resistance. History is not an objective scientific record. Bill Ashcroft says, "The link between representation and misinterpretation alerts us to illusoriness of historicity. [. . .] The question of truth or fiction of history may be best resolved in the concept of narrativity" (86).

A study of these three works raises the question whether a writer can change and distort the original text. Fiction as a literary genre gives ample scope to the free play of imagination. Bakhtin's definition of the novel quoted by Ken Hirschkop and David Shepherd in *Bakhtin and Cultural Theory* as an "intermingling of discourses, unified by the author's significant orchestration" (147), best described Tharoor's *The Great Indian Novel.* What is common to all the three novelists is that they have used the story of the *Mahabharata* to express their concerns about the afflictions of the times.

There have been many versions of the *Mahabharata* as well as the *Ramayana.* These retellings have many deviations and additions but they are true to the spirit and intent of the original. The fiction writers chosen for study go beyond this as they interrogate the original. This results in a next text, in a way a new epic. Each writer enjoys the freedom of the creative artist to alter the earlier works. Referring to his controversial work *The Satanic Verses* Salman Rushdie in "What is my single life worth?" stresses this aspect of the privilege of the creative artist:

> That even if my novel were incompetent, its attempt to retell the story would still be important. That if I have failed, others must succeed, because those who do not have power over the story that dominates their lives, power to retell it, rethink it, deconstruct it, joke about it and change it, as times change, truly are powerless because they cannot think new thoughts. (Mac Arthur 485)

It is this freedom and power to think new thoughts that distinguishes the creative artist from the rest of humanity. The new work that is produced can be seen as an extension of the older, or a new work in its own right or a text that subverts the original.

The very fact that fiction writers make use of a text that is part of the sacred lore of the land, to fit their own theoretical framework and get accepted shows the resilience that is characteristic of India. These books have not been banned as blasphemous. All the new thoughts emerging from the fictional rendering of the epic *Mahabharata* are related to the contemporary situation in India. In *India from Midnight to the Millennium* Tharoor makes an assessment of the contemporary situation in India. India continues to be a land of great resilience that has learned to cope with tragedy. According to Tharoor, "What can destroy India is a change in the spirit of its people away from the pluralism and co-existence that has been the greatest strength. [. . .] Equally there are vital areas of life, political and economic in which India cannot afford not to change" (323). Change is the law of life and law of nature.

The timeless epic has relevance for all societies at all times. The epic can be viewed as the story of the ruler and the ruled, the victor and the victim and the ideal and the real. There is a compelling need to set up ideal models, a need to communicate a message from the past. The present has to be altered by the past. T.S. Eliot in "Tradition and Individual Talent" says that the greatness of any artist depends on his relation to the tradition:

> No poet, no artist of any art has his complete meaning alone. His significance, his appreciation is the appreciation of his relation to the dead poets and artists. The existing monuments form an ideal order among themselves which is modified by the introduction of the new (the really new) work of art among them. (14)

The epics are the existing monuments that form an ideal order by themselves; but they are modified by the numerous attempts to re-render them in every age. The novelists adopt various devices such as selection, omission, addition, extension, deviation and distortion, in appropriating the epic to the new context. Every such attempt produces a new work but its significance is only in relation to the original epic. All the three novels can be considered as new Bharatas or Mod-Bharatas in perfect harmony with the living tradition of the *Mahabharata.* There is no sense of an ending or closure in any of the works chosen for study; nor is there any dogmatic assertion of any single Truth. A pluralistic vision emerges in these novels. "The story of history itself is many stories, none of which has an end but all of which continue intersected and overlapping" (Ashcroft 111). An absolute Truth seems to be impossibility. Fluidity and temporality are paradoxically the constant aspects of life. Ancient India has shown ample evidence of the indefinable nature of Truth.

The epic *Mahabharata* has displayed the multidimensional aspects of human life with all its complexities. The problems in the contemporary India are not totally new to mankind. An earnest claim is made on behalf of the epic.

> *Dharme cārthe ca kāme ca mokse ca bharatarsabha!*
> *Yad ihāsti tad anyatra yan nehāsti na tat kvacit!!*
>
> In the realm of religion and ethics (dharma), of material progress and prosperity (artha) of the enjoyment of the pleasures of personal and social life (Kama) and of spiritual emancipation whatever is embodied in this epic may be found elsewhere; but what is not found in the epic, it will be impossible to find anywhere else.

Mukund Lath says, "We perceive ourselves with all our predicaments and questionings in the characters of this ancient epic as nowhere else in the entire expanse of Indian literature or perhaps that of any other ancient culture" (139).

This is evident in the findings of the novelists' interrogation of the epic. By recasting the events, reinterpreting the characters, deviating from the epic and distorting it, the novelists have grappled with the reality of the twentieth-century India. They have ended up by reasserting and reinforcing the relevance of the epic to any society at all times. Its perpetual contemporaneity is upheld by the writers and the values of the epic remain intact without suffering any reversal.

The *Mahabharata* is valued not because it has been traditionally so but because we need it to know ourselves and our situation. It is not merely the traditional attribution of veneration that keeps it alive but its continuing relevance makes it a living tradition.

Bibliography

Abel, Elizabeth, ed. *Writing and Sexual Difference,* Great Britain: The Harvester Press, 1982.

Allen Graham, *Intertextuality,* U.K. Routledge, 2000.

Ashcroft, Bill. *Post Colonial Transformation,* 2000. London: Routledge, 2001.

Aurobindo ,Sri. *On the Mahabharata.* Pondicherry: Sri Aurobindo Ashram Trust, 1991.

Balaswamy, P. "The Presence of the Past: Shashi Tharoor's *The Great Indian Novel* as Historiographic Metafiction," *Indian Literature Today,* ed. R.K. Dhawan, New Delhi, Prestige, 1994.

Barry, Peter. *Beginning Theory: An Introduction to Literary and Cultural Theory.* Manchester: Manchester University Press, 1995.

Bassnet, Susan & Trivedi Harish. *Post Colonial Transformation.* London: Routledge, 1999.

Beauvoir, Simone de. *The Second Sex.* Trans & ed. H.M. Parshley, 1949. London: Vintage, 1997.

Bharati Subramaniya C. *Kavithaigal.* 1981. Chennai: Bharathi Pathipagan 2000.

Bhargava P.L. *Retrieval of History* form Puranic Myths. Lucknow: Upper India Publishing House, 1984.

Bhyrappa, S.L. *Parva.* Trans. K. Raghavendra Rao. New Delhi: Sahitya Akademi, 1994.

Bloom, Harold. *The Anxiety of Influence: A Theory of Poetry.* London: Oxford University Press, 1973.

Bois, Page du. *History, Rhetorical Description and the Epic: From Homer to Spenser.* Cambridge: Brewer, D.S. Biblio, 1982.

Brunton, Paul. *A Search in Secret India,* Bombay: B.I., 1970.

Campbell, Joseph. *The Hero with a Thousand Faces.* 1949. London: Fontana Press, 1993.

Chaitanya, Krishna. *The Mahabharata: A Literary Study.* New Delhi: Clarion Books, 1985.

Chandra Bipan, et. al. *India's Struggle for Independence:* 1857-1947. New Delhi: Penguin Book, 1987.

Chaudhury, M.K. "The Eternal Present: Shashi Tharoor's Story of India." *Recent Indian Fiction.* Ed. R.S. Pathak, New Delhi: Prestige, 1994.

Chellappan, K. "Archetypes in Indian Literature," *Triveni* 59.1 (Jan.-March 1990): 74-81.

Cuddon, J.A. *A Dictionary of Literary Terms.* Harmondsworth: Penguin, 1976.

Currie, Mark. *Post Modern Narrative Theory.* London: Macmillan, 1998.

Dandekar, R.N., ed. *The Mahabharata Revisited.* New Delhi: Sahitya Akademi, 1990.

Danino, Michel & Sujata Nahar. *The Invasion That Never Was.* Delhi: The Mother's Institute of Research, 2000.

Darshak, Manubhai Pancholi. *Kurukshetra.* (India, 1996). No Page.

Das, Manoj. "The Spell of the *Mahabharata.*" *Indian Express*, 31 December 1989.

Devahuti, ed. *Bias in Indian Historiography.* New Delhi: D.K., 1980.

Devy, G.N. "A Disappointing Novel," *Littcrit*, 16 1-2 (1990) 31-34.

Dhar, T.N "Entering History through the Backdoor: Tharoor's *The Great Indian Novel.*" *Commonwealth Novel in English* 7-8 (1997-1998) 125-47.

Dhawan, R.K., ed. *Indian Women Novelists.* New Delhi: Prestige, 1991.

_____. *Indian Literature Today*, New Delhi: Prestige, 1994.

_____ and Veena Noble, ed. *Fiction of the Nineties.* New Delhi: Prestige, 1994.

Dickman, Sue. Interview with Pratibha Ray. "In conversation," *The Book Review* 19.4: 30-35.

Dutt, M.N., ed. *Mahabharata.* 7 Vols. Delhi: Parimal, 1997.

Dutt, Romesh C. *The Mahabharata 1898.* New Delhi: Crest, 1995.

Eliot, T.S. *Selected Essays.* London: Faber and Faber, 1980.

Frawley, David. *Gods, Sages and Kings: Vedic Secrets of Ancient Civilization*, 1991 Delhi: Motilal Banarasidas, 1999.

Frye, Northrop. *Anatomy of Criticism: Four Essays.* 1957. Princeton: Princeton University Press, 1971.

Grassi, Maggi Lidchi. *Battle of Kurukshetra.* New Delhi: Roli, 1987.

_____. *The Legs of the Tortoise.* New Delhi: Roli, 1996.

Ghadially, Rehana, ed. *Women in Indian Society: A Reader*, New Delhi: Sage, 1988.

Hawthorn, Jeremy. *A Concise Glossary of Contemporary Literary Theory.* London: Edward Arnold, 1994.

Hirschkop, Ken & David Sheperd. *Bakhtin and Cultural Theory*, Manchester: Manchester University Press, 2001.

Hutcheon, Linda. *The Politics of Post Modernism.* London, Routledge, 1989.

James, Jancy. "*Mahabharata* as Draupadi's Tragedy: P.K. Balakrishna's Malayalam Novel, *Eni Njan Urangatte.*" *New Quest* 74 (Mar.-Apr. 1989): 87-94.

Karunakar, Supriya, "Games the Novelists Play: The Subversive Rebellion of Vikram Seth in *The Golden Gate* and Shashi Tharoor in *The Great Indian Novel,*" *Fiction of the Nineties.* Veena Noble & R.K. Dhawan, et. al. New Delhi: Prestige, 1994.

Karve, Irawati. *Yuganta: The End of an Epoch.* 1974. Hyderabad: Orient Longman, 1991.

Kaul, R.K. "*Mahabharata* Retold as an Epic of Modern India," *Indian Book Chronicle* 5.10 (1990):1.

Kermode, Frank. *The Classic.* London: Faber & Faber, 1975.

Khan, Hassan, "The Modern Re-Appropriation of Myth." *Alif Journal of Comparative Poetics.* 18 (1998): 174-204.

Kirpal, Viney. "Politics and Philosophy in *The Great Indian Novel,*" *Littcrit* 16.1-2 (1990): 45-54.

Kishwar, Madhu *Off the Beaten Track: Rethinking Gender Justice for Indian Women.* New Delhi: Oxford University Press, 1999.

Krishnamacharya, N.V.R. *The Mahabharata*, ed. M. Ramakrishna Sastry, Tirupati: T.T.D. Press, 1983.

Lal, P., ed. *Vyasa's Mahabharata: Creative Insights.* 2 Vols. Calcutta: Writers Workshop, 1992.

Lath, Mukund. "Understanding the *Mahabharata*: Irawati Karve's *Yuganta,*" *Indian Literature* 25.5 (1982): 134-49.

Lodge, David, ed. *Twentieth Century Literary Criticism: A Reader.* London: Longman, 1972.

MacArthur, Brian, ed. *The Penguin Book of Twentieth Century Speeches* 1992, London: Penguin, 1999.

Marathe Sudhakar, et. al. *A Way of Leaving So As to Say.* Chennai: T.R., 1994.

Matilal, Bimal Krishna, ed. *Moral Dilemmas in the Mahabharata.* Delhi: Motilal Banarasidas, 1989.

McLeod, John, 2000. *Beginning Postcolonialism.* Manchester: Manchester University Press.

Morris Pam. *Literature and Feminism: An Introduction.* Oxford: Blackwell, 1993.

Munshi, K.M. *Krishnavatara*. 7 Vols. 1962; Bombay: Bharatiya Vidya Bhavan, 1990.

Nair, M.T. Vasudevan, *Second Turn*. Trans. P.K. Ravindranath, Chennai Macmillan India, 1997.

Nandakumar, Prema. "Shashi Tharoor's Karna." *Littcrit* 16.1-2 (1990): 17-26.

Narayan, R.K. *The Mahabharata*. New Delhi: Vision, 1987.

Pandit, M.L. ed. *New Commonwealth Writing: A Critical Response*. New Delhi: Prestige, 1996.

Panikar, Ayyappa K. "Reminiscental and Subversive." *Littcrit* 16.1-2 (1990): 13-16.

Pathak, R.S., ed. *Recent Indian Fiction in English*. New Delhi: Prestige, 1994.

Prasad, Alok. "(Un)Intentionally (Un)Familiar." *The Book Review* 14.1: 41.

Quin, Edward. *Á Dictionary of Literary and Thematic Terms*. New York: Checkmark, 1999.

Rajagopalachari, C. *Mahabharata*. 1951. Bombay: Bharatiya Vidya Bhavan, 1999.

Rajan, P.K. "History and Myth in *The Great Indian Novel*." *Littcrit* 16.1-2 (1990) 27-31.

Rajaram, N.S. & David Frawley. *Vedic Aryans and the Origins of Civilization. A Literary and Scientific Perspective*. New Delhi: Voice of India, 1995.

Rao, M.S. *The Greatest Stories Retold, Ramayana and Mahabharata* UK: Horseshoe, 2000.

Ray, Pratibha, *Yajnaseni*. Trans. Pradip Bhattacharya. New Delhi: Rupa, 1995.

_____. "A Writers Pain, and Pleasure—Some Meandering Reflections." *Indian Literature*. 35.3 (May-June 1992): 140-51.

_____. Interview. "The Real and the Spiritual." *Indian Literature*. 39.2 (1996): 125-35.

_____. Interview. "Voice of the Voiceless." *Malayalam Literary Survey* 22.2 (April-June 2000): 87.

Ramakrishnan, E.V. "The Politics of Languages and the Language of Politics: Anita Desai's *In Custody*, Shashi Tharoor's *The Great Indian Novel* and O.V. Vijayan's *The Saga of Dharmapuri*. *Littcrit* 16.1-2 (1990): 55-69.

Rice, Philip & Patricia Waugh, ed. *Modern Literary Theory*. London: Edwin Arnold, 1989.

Richman, Paula, ed. *Many Ramayanas*. Delhi: Oxford University Press, 1991.

Salat, M.F. "Shashi Tharoor's *The Great Indian Novel*," *Contemporary Indian Fiction in English*. Ed. Avadesh K. Singh. New Delhi: Creative, 1993.

Sawant Shivaji, *Mrityunjaya*. Trans. P. Lal. Calcutta: Writers Workshop. 1989.

Schneir, Miriam, ed. *The Vintage Book of Feminism*. New York: Vintage, 1994.

_____. *The Vintage Book of Historical Feminism*. 1972; London: Vintage, 1996.

Scott, Wiber. *Five Approaches of Literary Criticism*. New York: Collier, 1962.

Selden Raman. *A Readers' Guide to Contemporary Literary Theory*. Lexington: The University Press of Kentucky, 1985.

_____. *Practising Theory and Reading Literature: An Introduction*. London: Harvester Wheatsheaf, 1989.

Sethuraman, V.S., ed. *Contemporary Criticism: An Anthology*. India: Macmillan India, 1989.

_____. "Literature after Theory: A Case Study." *Indian Journal of American Studies*. 23.1(1993): 29-34.

_____. "Resonance & Intertextuality." *A Way of Leaving So as to Say*. Ed. Marathe Sudhakar, et. al. Chennai: T.R., 1994.

_____. *Shriman Mahabharatam*. Delhi: Nag, 1998.

Sidhanta, N.K. *The Heroic Age of India*. India: Asian Publishing Services, 1997.

Singh, Avadesh K. *Contemporary Indian Fiction*. New Delhi: Creative, 1993

Sivasankari. *Knit India through Literature*. Chennai: East West, 2000.

Spence, Lewis. *Introduction to Mythology*. 1921. London: Senate, 1994.

Srinivasan, Seetha. "In Search of an Identity," *The Hindu*, 25 August 1991: 1.

Srenski Iran. *Four Theories of Myth in Twentieth Century History*. Iowa: University of Iowa Press, 1987.

Sukthankar, V.S. *On the Meaning of the Mahabharata*. Delhi: Motilal Banarasidas, 1998.

Thakur, M.M. *Thus Spake Bhisma*. Delhi: Motilal Banarasidas, 1992.

Thapar, Romila. *Exile and Kingdom Some Thoughts of Ramayana*. Bangalore: The Mythic Society, 1987.

_____. *Interpreting Early India*. Delhi: Oxford University Press, 1992.

Tharoor, Shashi. *The Great Indian Novel.* New Delhi: Penguin, 1989.

_____. *India: From Midnight to Millennium.* India: Penguin, 1997.

Thomas P. *Indian Women through the Ages.* New Delhi: Asia, 1964.

"Timeless Classic of Jason Revisited." *The Hindu Business Line* 8.9209 July 2001.

Tripathi, Vanashree. "Polysemy at the Dead End: Shastri Tharoor: *The Great Indian Novel." Recent Indian Fiction*, ed. R.S. Pathak. New Delhi: Prestige, 1994.

Varma, Pavan K. *Yudhishtar & Draupadi.* Viking Penguin, 1996.

Wheeler Kathleen & C.T. Indra. *Explaining Deconstruction.* India: Macmillan, 1997.

Woolf, Virginia. *A Room of One's Own.* 1929. England: Penguin, 1967.